Eating
WITH YOUR
Anorexic

Eating
WITH YOUR
Anorexic

*How My Child Recovered
Through Family-Based Treatment and
Yours Can Too*

Laura Collins

McGraw·Hill

New York   Chicago   San Francisco   Lisbon   London   Madrid   Mexico City
Milan   New Delhi   San Juan   Seoul   Singapore   Sydney   Toronto

Library of Congress Cataloging-in-Publication Data

Collins, Laura, 1961–
Eating with your anorexic : how my child recovered through family-based
treatment and yours can too / by Laura Collins.—1st ed.
    p.   cm.
  ISBN 0-07-144558-7
    1. Anorexia nervosa—Popular works.   2. Anorexia in children—Patients—
Family relationships.   3. Parent and child.   4. Parenting.   I. Title.

RC552.A5C655   2005
618.92′85262—dc22   2004015654

1 2 3 4 5 6 7 8 9 0   FGR/FGR   3 2 1 0 9 8 7 6 5 4

ISBN 0-07-144558-7

McGraw-Hill books are available at special quantity discounts to use as premiums and
sales promotions, or for use in corporate training programs. For more information,
please write to the Director of Special Sales, Professional Publishing, McGraw-Hill, Two
Penn Plaza, New York, NY 10121-2298. Or contact your local bookstore.

Nearly all the names in this book, including the author's, have been altered or changed
to protect the privacy of the family.

This book is printed on acid-free paper.

For my fierce, funny, and beloved daughter

CONTENTS

FOREWORD

IT WAS NOT TOO LONG AGO that when I began working with a teenager with anorexia nervosa, I told parents it was important for them to stay in the background and let me try to treat the adolescent without much parental involvement. I had been taught that adolescents with eating disorders were likely victims of parents overcontrolling them and that the only avenue left to them to experience independence was through food and weight. In many ways, this appeared to be true. Generally, parents were very anxious about their child and they often appeared both intrusive and overprotective—just as I had been taught they would be. No wonder their son or daughter needed a way to get away. In addition, when we admitted the adolescents to hospitals, which removed their parents from the day-to-day struggles over food and eating, we found that most adolescents gained weight and ate more normally. However, when they were discharged from the hospital and returned to their parents' care, they lost weight and began their preoccupations with food, exercise, and weight once again. Often they came back to the hospital in worse shape than we sent them out. Surely then, William Gull, the English physician who first described anorexia nervosa, was right about "parents being the worst attendants" for their children.[1] Salvadore Minuchin—an early family therapist—was also on the mark when he claimed that family processes were severely disturbed in those families wherein a child developed anorexia nervosa.[2] Further, it appeared those clinicians who advocated for "parentectomy" as a treatment for anorexia nervosa were likely on to something.

I discovered, however, somewhat slowly and belatedly, that something was wrong with eliminating parents from treatment. I began to question these professional opinions about parents and how best to treat anorexia nervosa because of a study that was published in 1987—a study that, unfortunately, received far too little attention.[3] That study, one of a handful of studies of treatment of anorexia nervosa to include adolescents, found that a treatment that presumed parents could help their children recover was superior to a treatment that focused on the individual adolescent. True, it was a small group of adolescents who were studied and there were a variety of ways the study's design (like almost all such studies) could be criticized, but the finding that parents could be a resource to help their children seemed genuine. Importantly, these researchers followed up their young subjects five years after treatment and found that 90 percent had fully recovered, significantly greater than the percentage of those who had received individual therapy. My curiosity was piqued, and I wanted to make sense of this surprising discovery.

The use of parents as a resource for their child's recovery as presented in that 1987 study was developed at the Maudsley Hospital in London by Christopher Dare, a child psychiatrist, psychoanalyst, and family therapist, and Ivan Eisler, a child psychologist and family therapist. The treatment was innovative in many ways. Not only did the treatment focus on parents taking charge of refeeding their underweight teenager, but it also disregarded the commonly suggested cause of the development of anorexia—that parental or familial pathology was at the root. Dare and Eisler took an "agnostic" position as to the etiology of anorexia nervosa because, they said, science had yet to determine its cause and to presume that parental or familial pathology is at the root of it is to lay blame and induce guilt without clear evidence of the accuracy of this claim. Most scientists believed it was typically the parents' fault, but Dare and Eisler felt the family dynamic did not have to be deemed dysfunctional just because a child had an eating disorder.

Studies that suggest parents cause anorexia nervosa are fraught with difficulty. First, there have been studies that have suggested correlations between family dysfunction as well as ones that have not. Importantly, none of these studies was conducted prior to the onset of anorexia and therefore does not take on the real effect of the illness on parents and families. We know that the advent of a serious illness affects family and parental functioning; without the proper study we cannot know if that dysfunction was there prior to the illness or if it was a result of it. A study was published a few years ago that evaluated the symptoms of anxiety and trauma that persisted in childhood cancer survivors. The researchers found that the children (who personally experienced surgeries, medications, isolation, and pain) had little evidence of residual effects of their treatment; in contrast, parents were found to still be much affected by their child's ordeal and suffered from intrusive memories, anxiety, and dreams about the suffering of their children many years after the fact. The point is that parents, understandably, in the throes of a life-threatening illness such as cancer or anorexia nervosa, are not likely to be functioning in a typical manner. Indeed, it would be surprising if they were not anxious, intrusive, and overprotective.

Dare and Eisler also emphasized early symptomatic control—that is, refeeding and weight gain—in their treatment approach. This focus arose in part from their experience as clinicians on an inpatient ward where nurses fed severely malnourished adolescents with anorexia nervosa. They noticed that adolescents who were eating and gaining weight were more likely to participate in treatment and make progress in recovery. They also noted, correctly, that medical staff, not the adolescent, were in charge of refeeding, at least initially, and felt that it was possible that parents could learn to do this at home and thereby save their child and family the painful disruption of hospitalization. It was not until later in treatment that the adolescent was asked to take up eating on his or her own, and then only under parental supervision and guidance, as would have been the case on a long-term inpatient unit. They focused their treatment on issues of adolescent control and autonomy only when the symptoms of anorexia nervosa abated sufficiently that these concerns could be addressed without the interference and distraction that self-starvation imposed on family and individual functioning.

When I read about the type of treatment Dare and Eisler had used in the study, I recognized that it turned typical treatment for anorexia nervosa on its head. Instead of focusing on what supposedly causes anorexia, treatment begins with getting eating and weight normalized before turning to psychological issues. This approach to treatment made sense to me. After all, that was exactly what we did in our inpatient service. Still, the notion of putting the parents in charge of refeeding seemed a stretch to me. Parents told me many times that they had tried to force-feed their child to no avail. I believed them. Our team of professionals, including a pediatrician, nurses, nutritionists, and various types of therapists, had enough difficulty accomplishing refeeding. But as I said, I couldn't ignore the tantalizing bit of evidence of another, perhaps more effective way of helping my patients with anorexia nervosa. If Dare and Eisler were right, then it might be possible to help patients with anorexia nervosa with less hospitalization and specialty care— something that is hard to find in any event. It happens that just as I began to be interested in this treatment, two additional small studies, also conducted at the Maudsley Hospital, that employed an approach of family-based treatment—what has come to be called the Maudsley approach—were published. These studies were again of adolescents, but this time they were treated exclusively as outpatients, and the vast majority appeared to recover without having to be admitted into an intensive inpatient program to refeed them.

My own work with family treatment based on the Maudsley approach began in 1998 when I received an NIH grant to conduct a treatment trial at Stanford University for anorexia nervosa using Dare and Eisler's family treatment model. The study began by working with Dare, Daniel Le Grange, Ph.D., and W. Stewart Agras, M.D., to distill the treatment into a manual that therapists could use consistently across all the families they treated.[4] This manual also allowed Dare and Eisler's treatment to be used in a study outside the Maudsley Hospital, this time in the United States, for the first time. As I began piloting the treatment using the approach and working with families, it quickly became evident to me that my initial hesitations were largely unfounded. Although most parents had tried to help their children eat, they were understandably initially perplexed about how to do it, worried they would do the wrong thing, and lost confidence. Eventually they gave up and felt defeated by anorexia. However, with an expert consultant to help them think through the dilemmas and to evaluate options, as well as to encourage persistence in the face of opposition, I found, as did the therapists who worked with me, patients improved under their parents' care and most did so relatively quickly.

Over the past six years, we have discovered that most patients whose families undertake family-based treatment as developed by the Maudsley group improve dramatically. Of course, there are exceptions to this, and for reasons that still elude us, 20 to 30 percent of families struggle to make a success of the approach.

When we started our work, there were few places parents might go to find ways they could be involved in helping their child.[5] Laura Collins's book, *Eating with Your Anorexic*, is now poised to dramatically correct this deficiency. When she and her husband became frustrated with treatments for their daughter, they went searching for information about the Maudsley approach. Based on their experiences, she wrote this book, which chronicles how she and her husband learned about anorexia nervosa, how they came to believe that their direct involvement with their daughter's recovery would be more beneficial than traditional treatments, how they struggled to find their way to help their daughter, and how they succeeded in defeating this devastating illness that appeared to have an intractable hold on their child. In clear, intelligent, and inspiring prose, Ms. Collins takes us on a journey of discovery that discloses the very parental ingenuity, patience, intelligence, persistence, and love that the Maudsley approach leverages to such effect in helping parents successfully aid their children with anorexia.

Eating with Your Anorexic will be a valuable resource to both parents and clinicians who wish to understand better the issues parents face when their child has an eating disorder, as well as to appreciate parental aptitude for learning and succeeding even in the face of incredible odds. I like to say that defeating anorexia nervosa is like climbing a sand hill: you can't rest until you get to the top or you will slide right back down again. Collins's book will inspire you on the climb and will give you some ideas that will increase the likelihood you will reach the top.

—*James Lock, M.D., Ph.D.*
    Associate Professor of Child Psychiatry and Pediatrics,
    Stanford University School of Medicine, and Director
    of the Eating Disorders Program at Packard Children's
    Hospital at Stanford

1. Gull, W. "Anorexia Nervosa (Apepsia Hysterica, Anorexia Hysterica)." *Transactions of the Clinical Society of London* 1874 (7): 222–28.
2. Minuchin, S., B. Rosman, and I. Baker. *Psychosomatic Families: Anorexia Nervosa in Context.* Cambridge, MA: Harvard University Press, 1978.
3. Russell, G. F., G. I. Szmukler, C. Dare, and I. Eisler. "An Evaluation of Family Therapy in Anorexia Nervosa and Bulimia Nervosa." *Archives of General Psychiatry* 1987 (44): 1047–56.
4. Lock, J., D. Le Grange, W. S. Agras, and C. Dare. *Treatment Manual for Anorexia Nervosa: A Family-Based Approach.* New York: Guilford Publications, Inc., 2001.
5. Lock, J., and D. Le Grange. *Help Your Child Beat an Eating Disorder.* New York: Guilford Press, 2004.

1

HOW TO GET FIRED
BY YOUR THERAPIST

THE THERAPIST FIRED US for insubordination.

Of course, it should have been us firing her. For the bland CD loop that breathlessly harassed us in the tiny and noncommittal waiting room. For the use of jargon as if it were English. For the fifty-minute hours, the $1.80 minutes, and the careful, therapeutic smile as she took the check.

My husband and I dragged our fourteen-year-old daughter to this place weekly because she lost twenty-one pounds in seven weeks, her body couldn't maintain its temperature, and her pulse had lowered to the threshold of sudden heart attack— something about her thighs being too big. In the last two months we had already careened through four therapists, ducked one hospital admissions staff, worn out our pediatrician, and annoyed a highly regarded dictician. Now we were being fired.

I should have been horrified, scared, or at least contrite. What does it mean when the professional you once begged for help suddenly sends you packing?

But the truth is that it was a great gift. Being fired may have saved my daughter's life.

Because she was getting better. And no one seemed to like that.

IN THE SUMMER OF 2002, when our epicurean daughter stopped eating, my husband and I turned to a succession of specialists and eating disorder professionals for help. Our daughter, Olympia, living in a malnutritious haze, wanted no help and admitted no problem. But we did what every book, pamphlet, and Public Service Announcement advises desperate parents to do when confronted with a child with an eating disorder: get help, get specialized help, do it now.

After nine weeks of therapy (and nine more pounds lost) we asked for a meeting with our eating disorder specialist, Joy. She said it without flowers: "I've never had anyone ask me these questions before."

I was, indeed, asking a lot of questions. After recovering from the initial shock, I wanted to know why my daughter woke up one summer day with a conviction that eating food was the moral equivalent of a heroin addiction. I wanted to know what we were doing wrong and how to fix it. I brought my daughter to the center to get help, and I wanted to find out what, exactly, they did there.

"I don't think you trust me," said Joy.

Maybe we didn't. We were not sure whom to trust anymore. Certainly not ourselves. It was a new experience for us to leave our child with a stranger with whom there were to be no secrets, yet from whom we heard little. We are the kind of parents who read food labels, insist on meeting the parents of our children's friends, and attend parent-teacher night. I wasn't adjusting well to being the outsider in my daughter's care. I was not being a good patient-mother.

I had gotten the notion that part of my role as parent was to understand and support the philosophical underpinnings of our daughter's care, as one does for an ear infection or the odd rash, and so I did my homework. I went for extra credit. I downloaded, cross-referenced, sent away for, and read everything with the key words *anorexia* and *nervosa*. I read books not meant for mere mothers. And I had questions, lots of questions.

But Joy's patient was our Incredible Shrinking Daughter, and we were only the people with the rapidly shrinking bank account. Our parental questions were not part of Joy's job description. Her answers—to us—were obviously not part of the treatment "modality." In fact, I was getting the feeling we were not seen as necessary at all.

In the rude awakening that is anorexia nervosa, we were learning that parents are not welcome. Mom and Dad are sent to a separate room, given $50 seminars on the influences of the media, and told to double-check on the family insurance coverage. Not only were we not welcome in our daughter's therapy sessions, we were advised to stay out of her recovery.

And under no circumstances were we to feed her.

I asked why.

"Whoa!" said Joy. "Aren't you getting a little too . . . involved?"

As if that is not what parents do. As if it were some sort of new symptom. Joy spoke as if she knew things I did not, could not, and should not know. I blinked. My world had shifted. It turned out that by bringing our daughter for help we had turned ourselves in for a crime of which we were unaware, as though we'd shown up at Social Services pointing out the bruises we inflicted on our own child's head. Having brought Olympia to them, we were to be penitent and obedient, as guilty parties must. Our daughter was in charge now, empowered by her enigmatically smiling therapist. We were not in a position to ask questions—and certainly not to have opinions.

One day we were a frazzled, busy, happy family leading normal lives. Our daughter was the envy of our friends, the easy child, the mature child, the one with such potential. One day later our child was ill with delusions that would cause her to deplete her vital organs and drain away the margin that keeps us safely among the living. The daughter with whom I had shared so much became emotionally unavailable. Her intellect faded in and out. And I was completely baffled to be told to stay out of it.

If she woke up one day believing that she was Napoleon, we and all the doctors and relatives and therapists and other unindicted co-conspirators of this story might have reacted more quickly or with more alarm. We would have seen it for the hallucination it was. But anorexia so closely resembles the madness of American womanhood that I think we all found it difficult to distinguish. Suicide, when it looks like dieting, just seems to earn you respect.

As the parent of an anorexic, your demotion as authority figure is instantaneous. Anorexia nervosa is a damning symptom of which you, the parent, are the cause. The only thing left is to identify the mode of your sin. No one tells you much of anything. You live with her, but you are suddenly irrelevant, pushed to the side, expected to be quiet. My daughter's chart noted my body size, my level of anxiety, my level of engagement.

Good parents are supposed to stay involved, engaged, and informed. Parents of anorexics are supposed to distance themselves. Let's do the math. Parents who bring their children in for evaluation for eating disorders are instantly suspect. So what, I wonder, are we to think of the parents who don't?

Sometimes I wish I were one of them.

2

"YOU SHOULD PROBABLY EAT MORE"

THE PEDIATRICIAN THOUGHT Olympia should eat more.

"How's the appetite?" she asked, eyes fixed on the thickening chart and avoiding my dwindling daughter. I hung my head.

Anorexia isn't about appetite, of course. My daughter was hungry. She was desperately hungry. She talked about food all day. Her room was layered with *Gourmet, Bon Appétit, Martha Stewart Holidays*, and most of the cookbooks in the house. She collected recipes from the newspaper, from magazines, off the Internet, from friends. A talented artist, she now drew only vivid, succulent fruits—her best work to date. There were notebooks lying around the house filled with pages of menus for "the perfect meal."

Not that she ate anything, but she sure talked about it. Until, horrified, we made her stop, she would cook elaborate dishes for us and watch us eat them. She could recite for each of us every bite of every food eaten by everyone in the house for successive days. She kept track of every other diner in a restaurant, tracing the forks from plate to lips like a besotted lover.

If her little brother asked for a snack she sprang up before we could, as if we were neglecting him. "He's hungry!" she would say with cruel reproach.

This is how the starving act. Her appetite was fine. I, however, became a bit queasy.

EATING IS ONE OF THE basal needs and desires of the human condition. The Chinese politely ask, "Have you eaten?" instead of "How are you?" The call to the table in many languages translates as "good appetite." If you don't eat, you won't reproduce, and the evolutionary mill will toss you out of the gene pool.

A group of conscientious objectors during World War II were asked to be part of an experiment to study the effects of starvation. Thirty-six men voluntarily consumed a semistarvation diet and lost 25 percent of their body weight. They, too, became obsessed with recipes. The men also temporarily lost their social abilities and their interest in social engagements and sex. One started shoplifting. Another compulsively searched through garbage cans. One chopped off three fingers. After the exercise was over, many had trouble getting their health back. Some were haunted emotionally by their starvation experience, and those living still have reunions. This was no simple experiment.

Very few people can fast to the death. I find myself wondering how many of those who do are actually anorexics in a righteous disguise. I see with new eyes the phenomena of political fasting, of religious fasting, of Buddhists living on breath. To suppress this most basic of needs is to strangle oneself—more slowly, but no less effectively, than poison, a blade to the artery, a bullet aimed at the brain. Fasting to starvation, in pursuit of a cause or out of illness, does a great violence to the body that—for the survivor—has consequences that are not repaired along with the regaining of simple body fat.

Starvation, which can technically be called "chronic idiopathic progressive malnutritional hypophagia of environmental origin," is described in the *Columbia Encyclopedia* this way:

Condition in which deprivation of food has forced the body to feed on
itself. . . . First to be lost are fat deposits and large quantities of water. The
liver, spleen, and muscle tissue then suffer the greatest loss of weight. The
heart and brain show little loss proportionately. The starving person
becomes weak and lethargic. Body temperature, pulse rate, blood pressure,
and basal metabolism continue to fall as starvation progresses, and death
eventually ensues.

Choosing not to eat when you are hungry is not normal and it isn't healthy. Most people don't stop eating even when they are full. Anorexia, often treated as a matter of vanity or overeager dieting, is said to be eventually fatal for two out of ten victims and permanently disabling for 30 percent. Even those who are "cured" take years to do so. Twelve times more American females between fifteen and twenty-four die of anorexia nervosa than any other cause of death.

But for all the concerned arm-waving and earnest pamphlet distribution, Americans know little about eating disorders. Our pediatrician missed the classic signs of anorexia: dizziness, weight loss, body weight concerns, slowed heart rate, and dehydration. She said Olympia needed "more salt." Our daughter's coach was so startled by Olympia's fragile frame that she cried out when she hugged her, but the coach never called us. Her friends only admired her new shape. If our friends or neighbors or people on the street recognized the signs or behaviors, they said nothing to us. No alarms were sounded, no phone calls were made, not a word was uttered as her life was draining away.

An athletic person since she backflipped out of the womb, Olympia loved to exercise and challenge her body's limits. We always joked that she even watched television acrobatically. As a book-lifting family, we admired her continual sampling of new sports, challenges, and goals to achieve.

"I'm going to learn to cartwheel today," she'd say, and then she would.

Run a mile to celebrate her tenth birthday? I drove alongside.

Far from having to convince her to get up and out she dragged us out, got me moving, asked for more lessons, for soccer camp, for a ride to the track. Her healthy self-motivation was inspirational, admirable.

In the summer of 2002, Olympia trained intensively in tae kwon do in preparation for the Junior Olympics in Knoxville that August. Samuel and I had never belonged to a sports team. We felt out of place among the other savvy athletic parents, but we were fully supportive, in our clueless way, of Olympia's determination to fit in and excel. Two weeks short of departure everyone who knew her felt her intensity, admiring it even as it worried us. It was her world, not ours, however, and we took her lead.

I was there in the room, but not looking, at the moment she fell. I, too, was trying to fit in and had finally made both eye contact and the beginning of a conversation with another parent who was explaining the mechanics of Olympic sparring. I had trouble watching my daughter being hit and punching back—it was the first day of such intense fighting and it scared me. I steeled myself to stand it if she could, to wince invisibly.

When I looked up, Olympia was on the ground. Someone was calling for ice. She was moved away from the action and practice resumed. I stayed where I was, watching the way people looked at me for instruction on how to react. One coach said to rest a moment and see. Another teammate said that the same thing had happened to her. Olympia was smiling, ready to go back in. At the time everyone was full of reassurances, but later they all said they heard the sound as the ACL (anterior cruciate ligament) snapped inside her knee.

Olympia went back in the ring once, but she couldn't stand. She insisted on coming back that evening to try again, and she did spar, briefly. Her coach insisted that it couldn't be the ACL, that Olympia "just rest." No one suggested a doctor.

That evening, unable to walk, she began exercising frantically with weights and a medicine ball. "I don't want to lose my conditioning," she said.

When I kissed her goodnight, leaving her downstairs, she was sweating with effort. I admired her moxie. How does one distinguish healthy determination from an unhealthy fixation?

"I should eat less, right?" she asked.

"What?" I said.

"While I'm not training, I'll need less food, right?"

Her tone annoyed me. It was so needy and strange. "Well, I guess you could eat a little less while you are stuck on your back. Just listen to your body."

She didn't respond.

It had probably started before the injury: eating less, exercising more. There were signs, but I was not listening for anorexia. That was a language I had never studied. I didn't hear that conversation at the time for what it was.

I HEAR IT NOW. I always will. But not her words. I hear my words: the permission, the magic words.

"Don't blame yourself." I can say it to others, but not to myself. What price would I pay to start again right there? I pay every day because I cannot.

Olympia stopped eating that day. And talking, really. It was like she left. She was so angry, so unaccepting of her twisted fate, so disappointed. We understood and we sympathized, of course. Her feelings seemed natural.

SURGERY WAS SCHEDULED for a few weeks later, but within a few days of the accident Olympia was on her feet again, riding an exercise bike for long, intense periods and acting strangely. She complained daily of feeling dizzy. She talked about eating and mealtimes as if they were of critical importance. But when it came to actually eating, there was always an excuse not to. The meal was too early or too late. It wasn't food she liked. It was too fatty or too much or too raw. She declared only two times a day suitable for eating: 10:00 A.M. and 7:00 P.M. She seemed extremely stressed, nervous, and angry. Before long, we felt the same way.

In the interest of distraction, we quickly arranged a vacation trip for the same week she would have left for Knoxville. For good measure, I brought her to the doctor again the day before we left, mostly because I was annoyed about her constant complaining about dizziness even while she ignored my advice to drink fluids and to eat more frequently. I knew she was suffering over the way the training had ended. I sympathized with her losses. I wanted the doctor's backup, a third-party opinion to get me out of the equation.

The medical records for that day, two weeks after her accident, note a weight loss and dizziness. She was prescribed "more salt" and fluids.

By the time we packed to return home from the trip it was clear that our daughter was terribly ill. Her obsession with mealtimes had become obvious. She was unable to speak rationally about anything involving food or her body. The dizziness was now constant and she confessed to once blacking out. She became angry when confronted with food, nervous when mealtimes approached, and physically ill and frightened after consuming anything.

On the ten-hour drive home, Samuel and I stared at the road ahead as though we were falling back to our house rather than driving. Beside her, Olympia had a two-inch stack of cooking magazines. She read each one, carefully, during the entire drive. She fed her brother from the cooler full of snacks packed for the ride, but she did not eat. Aside from Elijah's calls for more snacks between video games, the only sound in that car was magazine pages being turned.

The day we returned, I scheduled an appointment between the pediatrician and me. I said I believed Olympia was anorexic. I laid out the symptoms, the irrational behaviors and thoughts. Then I brought my daughter, under protest, to the office. This time I was sure I would get the solid backup we needed to convey the seriousness of the situation to this recalcitrant child.

"You should probably eat more, but you are still doing all right," the doctor said.

Olympia actually smiled.

That conversation still astonishes me. The front line, primary care foot soldier had, in one sentence, brushed away my daughter's trust in my judgment and my trust in the doctor's office. My daughter heard she was "all right" and I heard "you are on your own." I have since heard this identical story from other parents. Even doctors don't understand eating disorders.

When we did confess—only to those who absolutely had to know—that it was anorexia, we discovered that this well-known disease is everything but. And unlike other diseases that need attention in order to raise funds, anorexia needs to be known for another reason entirely: in this case, ignorance kills.

Our ignorance could have killed our daughter.

3

WHO ARE YOU CALLING WHITE, WEALTHY, AND GREAT IN SCHOOL?

"I AM NOT ANOREXIC."

My daughter is not exactly white and not very wealthy, but in this one data point of the anorexia demographic she fills the bill: she's a good student.

That's my fault. I believe in working hard in school. I think that poor grades are a waste of time and that education is a precious gift. I think that good scholarship should be rewarded, that As should be deserved, and that "social promotion" is like flushing a toilet. I believe that educated people get more out of life, and that, regardless of one's life path, knowing more is better than knowing less.

You'd ask me for my tips on parenting if my daughter got into Harvard but not if she got anorexia. I obviously pushed her too hard. Oh . . . *that* kind of mother. You know the type.

Olympia skipped first grade because she could already read. She's self-motivated and competitive. She read early and a lot. At eight she memorized the American presidents in order. She knows the characters on "The Simpsons" and in *Macbeth*. A smart kid with varied interests.

She collects gourmet recipes. She knows the functions of the major vitamins and the chemistry of baking. She reads food labels.

But in the August before her sophomore year, this smart girl began to believe that 1,000 calories was too much food for one day. If she ate breakfast she felt unentitled to lunch. She referred to water as good and bread as bad.

If it were little green men she saw, we would know what was delusion and what was not. Our family's anorexia awakening lacked that clarity.

I still wish it were little green men; I think they have a pill for that. And even if they don't, that sort of delusion isn't life-threatening. She could join a support group or start a newsletter. Eccentricity you can live with.

But this thing that was happening to her—that happened so suddenly and completely changed her—this wasn't benign or a curious phase. This was horrifying and immediate and scary. The girl we knew was no longer there, no longer rational, although we tried to treat her as if she were. Her mind and her body were fading as if her life's blood were being drained away. In fact it was.

We all know the stereotype of anorexics: white, upper-middle-class, high-achieving girls. Those are the polite demographics. Now let's say what we really think. Anorexics are freakish sideshow characters. They are nervous, shifty, vain creatures who incite that envy that none of us like to admit. They just go a little too far is all. We love the skinny ones until one day we think "anorexia," and then we see them as tainted, strange, and embarrassing. Not people we'd want our children to hang out with or our daughters to be influenced by. Like abuse victims—we feel real bad for them but, you know, after that . . .

And the parents! Nervous types. The distant and volatile fathers who can't show affection. The strained, thin mothers who oh-so-pointedly suggest that their daughters lose a few pounds. Hypocritical mothers on diet pills reliving their glory days or lost opportunities through their cheerleader children. Dysfunctional families with hidden perversions, secrets, probably drinking or pills. The kind of people you love to see fall—which they will—but you feel sorry for the kids. And you're glad when they move away so you can talk openly behind their backs.

You can admit it. We all know what you are thinking. We've all felt it. I don't mind.

But there's a problem. That family is not us.

On a superficial level, I guess we fit the part. We are a normal, unremarkable family. Our little nuclear unit with a mortgage and a minivan looks average. We could easily pass a credit check or a security check, and we cut our lawn regularly. Our ash-blonde daughter looks the part of an "After-School Special" anorexic: she's pretty, good in school, well dressed. We're educated, we read a lot of books, we keep up with the news. Our bills are paid and we contribute to our 401(k).

But really, you can't cram us into the profile very neatly at all. Life is complicated. We are middle class but this is a very recent event. We look white, but my birth certificate says "Negro" and we straddle Judaism and atheism with a lot of athletic multiculturalism. Throw in some Mediterranean and Native American and an extended family more diverse than the United Nations and there we are.

We aren't hiding any juicy dysfunctions. No drugs, no criminal past. Samuel and I fall asleep after two glasses of wine. Our marriage is healthy, our parents are living, and our childhoods were undramatic. Our two children have lived happy, home-based lives with loving parents and an abundance of doting grandparents. Aside from some asthma and a few allergies, we are healthy.

Anorexia, however, made what was normal suddenly suspect. If we were ambitious, we were too ambitious. If we were casual, we must really be neglectful. If we were good parents, we must be too good, somehow. Something was clearly wrong: with us, with her, with us and her.

The books, the pamphlets, the websites, and the people we consulted gave few answers about what to do but provided us with plenty of questions: Who abused her? (Is it still going on?) Is this mother too controlling? (Too cold?) How does the father play into this? (Why isn't he here today?) Does the mother diet? (Hmm.) Were the children forced to clean their plates? What magazines have you bought her? How much television do you let her watch? Are there male relatives with access to her? Are you serious when you say you don't believe she lies to you? What about drugs? Is she on birth control? When did you stop beating your daughter?

Normalcy was no excuse. With a disease that kills and maims with the savagery of this one, it was not going to be normalcy that saved us.

4

"EVERYONE EATS!"

"You have to eat," I said with borrowed enthusiasm. "Everyone eats."

Rationalizing eating was a new experience for me. I never thought of eating as optional, nor did I know anyone who thought that. The necessity of eating is so obvious I had never devised an argument for why you must, several times a day, nourish yourself.

When eating became optional—and then unnecessary—to Olympia, I struggled to talk her out of the anorexia. Her withering dismissal of my bright parental insights had all the authenticity of any teenager tolerating a clueless adult. She did not need to say anything. She knew that people didn't eat. And throughout those first days, and then weeks, of trailing behind her, terrified and confused, I fought a losing battle. The world showed her she was right—over and over.

Ubiquitous diet product commercials mocked me. The dieting detritus in our kitchen undermined me: chromium picolinate pills, protein powder, Equal, stevia drops. Unknowing people wounded me everywhere we went with the steady rain of excuses, admonitions, apologies, and regrets of normal conversation:

"I feel *so* guilty about this extra slice," a guest insisted.

"I'm such a pig . . ."

A study came out in that first month of our anorexia hell that screamed "30 Percent of Americans Overweight" from large-font headlines and radio broadcasts. Olympia thought they were talking about her. She held up such stories as proof that I was the one who was irrational. My ministrations did not reach her. She seemed to feel sorry for me—under the condescension—for my ignorance. I didn't know whether to suck in my gut or loosen my belt. Everything I said was wrong. Everything I did was worse.

I tried calorie counting—in reverse. I still believed in her intellect, her common sense, the brain we had known and nurtured for more than fourteen years. I compiled a chart of her caloric intake for three successive days and looked up average energy needs. I overestimated the calories and underestimated the needs. She was interested at first, but finally dismissed it. On paper she was melting.

"You are not consuming enough to sustain your body. Every day you end up with a minus sign," I told her.

She didn't believe it. Logic meant nothing to her any more.

"You're not overweight!" I kept saying.

"It doesn't matter!" she kept saying. "Look at my thighs!"

It took me too long to realize it didn't matter how much she weighed or how hungry she was. She felt no better as she shrunk. She was no less tortured or more satisfied as meal after meal was bypassed. The situation quickly went from annoying to really frightening. And then my long-archived and repressed memories of pictures of anorexics suddenly became personal. It is not easy to take the precious child you know so well and respect so much and suddenly disregard everything she says. This child I had loved and taught and listened to was suddenly someone I could not listen to, must not listen to.

She spoke to me as if she were still herself, but she was not. I missed her already.

HOW DO YOU MAKE AN anorexic? Your recipe may vary, but here's how I made mine.

The infant Olympia only ate the finest baby foods. I know this because I prepared them myself. No canned applesauce, no preservatives, no Gerber mixed meats. Just steamed, hand-mashed, frozen-in-ice-cube-trays Olympia food. I breastfed her as though it were a religious calling, through two infections and many sleepless nights until it got easy. I expressed milk at the office, and carried it lovingly to the bemused babysitter who fed it to her while I was gone the next day. Breastfeeding went on for happy months until Olympia chose to wean herself.

I believed in a healthy, basic diet for babies. I believed in my baby's brain, her robust body, her immune system. I was feeding her her potential, her love of life, her love for me. I surrounded her with sensory delights, educational mobiles, and new experiences. I owed her the best I could give, based on the latest beliefs of child-rearing and nutrition. For this child, the best.

My progressive feeding philosophy was in line with that of Dr. Spock and the other fashionable experts of the era: provide a variety of foods, don't monitor quantities. Children will eat and enjoy a variety of foods. Don't let your own food preferences influence what you feed your children. Put out five wholesome things and don't worry about whether they like them. Feed them when they're hungry. Never push food on them. Don't make a fuss about food not eaten. Have lots of healthy snacks available. Don't make eating stressful. Carry crackers and fruit. Try new things. Try old things again. Mix colors. Have fun.

We did. I had so much fun watching her eat, letting her play with her food, seeing her squinch her nose at new things. I was a scientist, an explorer, an innovator. This parenting gig was turning out to be one of my better projects.

I lovingly laid out a variety of nonintuitive foods and then lovingly washed them off the white tile floor. I spent my evenings doing tiny laundry and preparing food in minute portions, making little baggies of serving-size chunks of peas, sweet potatoes, apples, squash. I remember those evenings as one remembers wrapping presents on Christmas Eve or sneaking a silver dollar under the tooth-baited pillow.

Food was fun, food was work, food was everywhere.

So I took credit, naturally, when my lovingly engineered child grew into a raging gourmand. This toddler was no cheap date. Although McDonald's would do for a night out with peers and Dunkin' Donuts on Friday mornings was our honored ritual, this kid preferred the good stuff. Raised on variety, she was game for Hawaiian, overjoyed at Nicaraguan, and eager to try Thai. Far from heading for the children's buffet, she sighed when faced with a plain cheeseburger or child-friendly fries. Bring on the tortellini with butter sage sauce and yes, she'd like to try the lobster . . . en croûte.

Olympia was an adventurous eater, an omnivore. She liked to eat at other people's houses. She liked to travel. She thought that Wednesday was the best day of the week because the *Washington Post* published the food section. She hated to eat the same thing twice in a row. She was not a snob. She rarely pouted or refused to eat something. She just appreciated good food and knew a lot about it. She ate with great pleasure, gusto, and a side of fries.

"What are they serving?" was her first question about an invitation.

"What did you eat?" was her first question about an event.

I USED TO FEEL RELIEF about Olympia's interest in cooking and food. It annoyed and embarrassed me that I do not cook well. My family was big on food as necessity and obligation, and our weekly turns at producing the required starch-green-protein were uninspired. Punctuality and getting it done were more important than taste or presentation. I compensated by learning four basic foods at a time—which, unfortunately, did not comprise a meal—and making them in ridiculous quantity. My potato latke fests are legendary, but I forget the applesauce. My Sabbath challahs are renowned, but I always make too much and they go stale. I routinely burn the last batches of cookies I ambitiously quadruple the recipe for. I'm a one-note cook and often off-key.

My daughter, on the other hand, was showing signs of being the competent one in the kitchen. That meant I had neither irretrievably ruined her nor was I to spend my last years eating cocktail wieners from the pop-top can: she would feed me.

I thought of her interest in cooking as a possible career direction and an asset in the housemate competition. It was another skill—of many— that made me thankful that biology is not really destiny: she was her own person.

What I feel now when I think of her bookshelf full of cookbooks, her *Bon Appétit* and *Gourmet* magazines, and her piles of recipe clippings is tricked. I feel guilty. I feel blind. I feel dumb.

Thirty-one percent of students in culinary schools are said to have an eating disorder. I didn't know that before and I'm sorry I know it now.

I NO LONGER KNEW WHETHER I should admire this once-overweening interest of my brilliant daughter. It looked now like the evidence of a long-brewing pathology or perhaps a once-promising talent now irretrievably tainted. Was she always an anorexic, or did her interest in food create a pathway for illness when it arrived? If I had been a better cook or made more dinners, been less incompetent in the kitchen, would some hunger of hers not have developed?

Samuel loved food. He ate without a schedule, without a plan, without any rules. He felt hungry, he ate. He preferred good food, but he wasn't going to turn down a hamburger. He had a dessert after breakfast, a sweet to finish lunch, and a bit of pie after dinner if he could find it. His childhood was filled with grandparents who fed you and peeled your grapes. He liked to eat. He didn't like to plan. Waiting for others to get hungry annoyed him. Making a grocery list or a meal plan for the week ahead exasperated him. Family meals, never a part of his childhood outside of holidays, seemed like an unnecessary bother. He enjoyed just eating. He thought we all should do the same.

Samuel and I searched our pasts and our books about anorexia to discern where we went wrong. We found plenty of ammunition. Our pasts as individuals and as parents now looked like laboratories of pathology. I had cared too little. My husband had cared too much. There was plenty of guilt to pass around. Extra helpings.

"Everyone eats," I insisted. But I lied. Everyone eats strangely.

5

TAKE THE FORK AWAY—
SHE'S NOT DONE YET

ANOREXIA IS DIAGNOSED when the following are true: you are 15 percent below a healthy body weight, you think you are overweight, and this has gone on for more than three months. The day before the three months are up, and at one pound over the limit, you are not "anorexic." Before that your family's hysterical pleading and bargaining and lectures are an overreaction. Before that you are "dieting." If you are shy of the threshold you are just "not ready" to get help.

At exactly three months your DSM-IV diagnostic designation ticks over the line, your insurance starts paying, and treatment centers start vying for your business. Step over the line and you get to be counted as one of the .05–3.5 percent of Americans with a verifiable, documented eating disorder.

As an added bonus, your eating disorder is especially lethal. Unlike those slacker binge eaters and mere bulimics, you have the most lethal mental disorder on the books. You are more likely to die of your disease than a schizophrenic or a manic-depressive. Since anorexics are notoriously competitive, you'll be pleased to learn that anorexics are sicker longer, hide their illness better, and have a variety of choices of ways to die. There is suicide, of course, or a sudden heart attack. You could slip away with an opportunistic infection from chronic malnutrition. The fragility of your bones from osteoporosis can cripple you or just give you a tangible precursor of the premature aging you will experience if you do live. If you live, your heart will be smaller, your other vital organs will be weakened, and you will always have a tendency toward obesity.

Ironically, you'll look like hell.

Anorexics, who generally begin by eating less, then eating ritually prescribed amounts, and rapidly end up eating nearly nothing at all, prolong the effects of involuntary starvation suffered by those who can't actually find any food. An anorexic's body has time to explore the many ways the human body can falter, and fail.

Even before you get really ill, however, ill enough to be called anorexic and compelled to get care, you will enjoy the benefits of your unique illness. You will experience a sense of cold that comes out of your bones. Your body, losing its ability to retain body heat, will be unrelievably chilled. Your lips may become blue.

If you are a successful anorexic—keeping a careful balance between starvation and death—your nails will chip off and your hair will break off near the scalp. A sign of your attentiveness to detail will be the furry layer of hair that will cover your body in a futile and atavistic effort to retain energy.

Very pretty.

Your breasts will hollow out; your eyes will protrude from your sinking flesh. On the bright side, you will no longer suffer from acne.

You will experience anemia, bruising, constipation, and insomnia, dental decay, bed-wetting, bacterial infections, blurred vision, and a depressed immune system. If you like big technical words, try on esophagitis, leukopenia, thrombocytopenia, and hypercarotinemia. If you keep it up, your kidneys fail and your heart stops.

None of what you are experiencing is caused by anorexia. They are all symptoms of starvation induced and enforced by the anorexic mind. In other words, an anorexic causes these symptoms by not eating. Imagine: if you are protected from restricting your diet, there are no physical symptoms at all. Your life is not physically in danger. Ask any eating disorder specialist and they'll tell you that anorexics who eat—the earlier the better—get better mentally, have a better chance of outliving their illness, and have a smaller chance of relapse. Starvation is the main deterrent to getting better mentally as well, because most of the symptoms of anorexia are caused by depriving the body of food. A diet, coincidentally, is how almost every anorexic starts their journey.

Despite these findings, you will be surprised to learn that food is not prescribed—or even advised in many cases—until the victim is physically diminished to the point of hospitalization. Yes, despite the macabre behaviors, the distorted thoughts, and the near inevitability of worsening prognosis, we still wait for anorexics to be so sick physically, regardless of their mental state, that they must be "refed" to survive. We wait until they "choose" to eat or until they are too sick to live.

Imagine us waiting for the words "Please, please help me!" in clear and correct English before jumping in to save a drowning person thrashing in the ocean. Since we define this mental illness through physical symptoms, we withhold critical care until such physical conditions are met. We define the illness as its symptoms and define cure as a temporary lack of death. It's no wonder, after recovery, anorexics often hate us.

All the physical and mental symptoms of anorexia are there before, and between, being called an anorexic. The diagnosis is about things that can be observed from outside of you: your weight, your electrolytes, your words. What you are feeling is impossible to measure as neatly as body mass index or a caliper to your thigh. Meanwhile, the mental hell you are experiencing is quite private, very much your own. You will need to get very ill before you qualify for more help than the neighborhood shrink can administer in weekly sessions, biweekly if you have enlightened insurance. Before you are officially anorexic you are just thinking wrong or thinking too much or thinking the wrong things or maybe avoiding thinking the wrong things.

"You cannot get well until you choose to get well," Olympia was told.

"You cannot make her well," we were told.

Our daughter's heart had slowed, temperature had dropped, and her skin was gray. She couldn't cry or describe any emotion and did not believe she was anorexic or any other kind of ill. Technically, she was right: she was not anorexic.

Like a pregnant girl isn't a mother. Like a jogger the day before his first heart attack. Like the Titanic at 11:39.

ANOREXIA MAY BE DIAGNOSED at a certain quantifiable level, but it is not a different animal the day before or after. I cannot tell you when anorexia starts, but it is not at diagnosis. I cannot say for sure how or whether it can be cured, but I am certain it is not when the victim decides to get well. But that is what they told us.

6

ROCK-THROWING LESSON #1

THROW A ROCK INTO A GROUP of mothers and I guarantee that you will hit a dieter. It is our national sport, consuming $35 billion of the American economy. If you are American and female you have most likely dieted.

We add foods, we subtract foods. We combine them in new ways. We supplement, remeasure, add condiments, subtract salt, slow-cook, find a new way of broiling, and start over in the morning. Lacking a national cuisine, we take everything, in any combination, and then condemn it. We are constantly renewed, refined, reformed. The gospels of food find penitents and true believers in a steadily renewable stream. Low-carb, high-soy, protein powder, lacto-ovo, watermelon-grapefruit, blood-type matching, Foreman style, ethnic correctness, organic politics—you are what you are seen eating. The season peaks after the holidays, but is moribund in December to let us fuel up for winter. The fashions change: protein to Zone, Swedish to Meridia.

I started late on this great American pastime. I knew that other people hated me, but I didn't care. I ate what I wanted, when I wanted, and my weight didn't vary. I was smug. I was standard height, standard weight. Weight concerns were for other people, other bodies. I was sympathetic to the angst of the overweight, but mostly oblivious. I winced at—and pretended to politely ignore—the grief that others seemed to attach to food. I regarded the diets of others like I did their astrology or their religion because I respected their right to diversity. Fat was cool. Skinny seemed fine. I was as vain as the next woman, but I preened over what languages I spoke and where I had traveled.

My first baby didn't change much. I switched to SlimFast for several meals a week after I stopped breastfeeding. The baby weight dropped and I went back to my old clothes. No big deal. I tried not to act smug. So that was what all the fuss was about. Losing weight wasn't so bad.

Diets or changing food habits are a form of discipline, right? You get out of control over a long period, you regain control. Nothing overnight, nothing temporary. People who had trouble dieting were consigned to my benign pity category, like high-functioning alcoholics and children whose parents watched too much TV. But I did note with silent pleasure that I was better.

THE SIGNS THAT I WAS OVERWEIGHT were a shock to me. I have the opposite of anorexia: I always feel thinner and better proportioned than I am. I've fluctuated forty pounds over ten years, mostly up, and never felt any different. I feel comfortable in my skin—even when it changes. From inside, I feel marvelous. Put the right dress on and I feel like a striking person, even an offbeat beauty some days.

I've wondered why Olympia didn't get this disorder of undeserved optimism from me. Which led me to wonder where the heck I got such delusions. Some day I suppose we'll select our children's genes from a catalog. I must remember to tell them that sometimes the broken parts are a good thing. A little constructive delusion can do a body good.

But of course it was my clothes that betrayed me. I started to notice sizes the day I realized that nothing in the regular sections of stores felt good on me. The next size up was the Plus area. Things chafed, or dug, or rode up on me. It wasn't the shape of the new fashions, it was my shape.

A few miscarriages, the approach to forty, and the complacency of a happy life had put a few pounds on me. I examined that broad standing next to my husband in family photographs and suddenly felt overweight in the eyes of others, though I resented it. I felt fat to my husband, who admitted that obesity was not one of his "turn ons." Being fatter felt not just older but less vital. I knew one could age gracefully but did not see myself growing fatter with elegance. For the first time I felt self-conscious about my body not out of modesty but out of embarrassment. My body, my old friend, was no longer on my side.

I'm not alone. Most mothers experience this. Most wives go through this. Most women know what I mean, eventually. I was late, but I got there. I had gained weight, too much weight, and it felt bad. I'm not good at feeling bad, so I resolved to change it, like I do all other problems. Losing weight and regaining my rightful self-esteem was like deciding to run a new business or make a career move: risky, a bit scary, but worth the effort. Doing nothing was not an option.

I was good at dieting. I have lots of discipline. I lost weight. I felt good about it. My twentieth high school reunion was a success: they said I hadn't changed a bit, and I believed them.

But with a slower metabolism I learned what everyone else does, that the body doesn't listen to my ego. It doesn't care about my discipline. Unless I was near starvation I would gain weight. When I ate too little I felt sadness like a howling moan that I couldn't relieve. My body's apparent set point was fifteen pounds above what I thought it "should be." I learned incontrovertibly what my precise dress size is and how to gauge my happiness by it. I learned what types of clothes suit what types of body. I learned that flexible waistbands are my friends and that short inseams are not.

Worst of all, I caught on to how people look at weight. I learned how humiliating fat is, how infantilizing being fat can be. I learned to feign disgust at skinny models and to envy the young. I noticed—now that I paid attention—how almost everyone around me described other people by their body weight and how closely that assessment was associated with respect, especially for women.

So when my daughter became anorexic I naturally blamed myself. The responsibility for her weight-consciousness pointed directly at me. She thought she was overweight—and that it mattered—and for some reason she was just taking it too far. Perhaps she misunderstood, I thought. Perhaps she saw me one too many times standing sideways to the mirror. She must have internalized some self-loathing, some deeper angst. After all, she wasn't getting fat, I was.

It occurred to me that most of us women of a certain age resolve to diet—and that we hit that certain perimenopausal age at the same time at which our pubertal daughters are most likely to begin an eating disorder. Some of this dieting is out of ridiculous ideals. Some of it is a flying gasp at retaining our youth. And we fail at it. We falter, we stumble. We go back to eating what we like, when we like. We lose our New Year's resolutions under the credit card bills. We sell the exercise equipment at a yard sale. We try again next year.

It was easy to blame my diets for Olympia's anorexia, but like all easy answers it was probably wrong. Anorexia nervosa is to dieting as decapitation is to a paper cut.

7

ROCK-THROWING LESSON #2

WHILE WE ARE THROWING rocks at easy targets, let's lob one at the crowd again. Let's close our eyes and see if we can hit a guilty mother.

I bet you got one on your first try.

Guilty for breastfeeding too little or too long.

For not being home with the kids or for being there too much.

For feeding too many bad or too few good things.

For keeping a messy house, and for not caring.

For marrying the father or for getting out while you still could.

For the kids having the wrong friends or too few friends or friends who treat them poorly.

For being too involved or too aloof.

For the time you spent and the time you didn't.

For being your mother and for not being your mother.

For being the only one, or the last one, or the youngest one, or the sloppiest one.

For caring about all those trivial things.

For not understanding how difficult parenting would be.

For having the hubris to think you'd do it better.

For discipline that didn't work or went too far.

For a world you cannot control, cannot hold off, cannot delay, and cannot stop.

For wanting to be alone sometimes.

Motherhood is a web of guilt, of responsibility, of being there. That's why we like it. And we wear it like a blue ribbon at every preschool "graduation," karate belt test, bar mitzvah, and school play. We are not to gloat, of course, but parenting is a hard job and we deserve to sit back and enjoy the benefits when our perseverance delivers the goods: a beaming child, an A-studded report card, the compliment of an older relative. We're proud of ourselves when we're proud of our kids.

And when things go wrong, it is our fault. We did it. The guilt is an all-you-can-eat buffet. We always knew we were bad parents. We always knew they'd see through us some day. It is a dress-up game, a fake—we were just playing along. Who let us have these kids, anyway? We're not qualified and we should have known better. We were too young, too stupid, or too hasty. It's our fault.

Our daughter was very ill. The rock hit us right in the face. But you have to wonder, was it aimed at us?

8

THE DISEASE THAT
SPEAKS ONLY ITS NAME

For a monster with such name recognition, anorexia nervosa is staggeringly misunderstood. The name is common, a tagline to a joke, spoken carelessly, unthinkingly, salaciously. It is prostituted for causes —feminism, psychoanalysis, a loathing of popular culture, scorn for petty women and their fatuous concerns—by advocates for the conservative family and by critics of modern living. We can all feed off it, rail against it, animate its analogies for our own purposes.

My only cause, as I started my sleepless nights of anorexia, was our daughter. Her dissolution as a corporeal being threatened to dissolve the ties of parent to child, brother to sister, husband to wife. It evaporated ties in concentric circles: friends, grandparents, neighbors, schoolmates, old friends, community. We drifted. Our family had a name now for the thief of our daughter's sanity, but that name meant little to us. We did not know what to do with this name except fear it. We did not know who to tell or who to consult. It meant so little to us because we had never really given it any thought.

The name became ours in an instant, before which I would never have considered it and after which there was no setting it aside. One vacation Olympia started annoying me again with her concerns about what she should eat and about her stomachache from eating a piece of pizza. For two days every "meal" had caused her a "stomachache." She said she should not be eating so much.

"I ate a whole slice."

"So?"

"I'm scared."

I faced her and said, "That's not rational." I was thinking more of the stress of the day, of all the relatives, of repacking the car, and of what Elijah was up to, but my attention was finally caught by the look of genuine fear in her eyes. In a bizarre and surreal moment, she pointed at her arms and said they were growing while she watched.

"That's crazy," I said. "Don't talk like that. That's disordered thinking." And my mind completed the thought: anorexia. Our lives cleave there, on either side of a word. Actually, two words: anorexia nervosa.

IT IS A MISNOMER, THIS NAME: *an* meaning "the lack of" and *orexia* meaning "appetite." Anorexics do not lack appetite, they are afraid of it. Anorexics fear hunger as well as satiation. The very topic of food is a gaping maw in which a gale-force storm is imminent. The *nervosa* part has a marvelous premodern feel to it and gives the impression that anorexics are hysterical and excitable. This too is untrue, as anorexia tends to render its victims almost mute and confers at some stages an unnatural calm.

There are other names to learn when you step over the line into anorexia. Medical and psychiatric journals prefer the term *anorectic* to describe the clinical symptoms of food restriction, distorted body image, and catastrophic weight loss.

There are even subspecies. Orthorexia nervosa describes anorexics who restrict by only eating health foods. Bigorexia is referred to as "antianorexia" and describes a mostly male phenomenon in which the body is perceived as too thin and weak. Anorexia is called "failure to thrive" in babies and "geriatric anorexia" in the elderly. Anorexia athletica sufferers exercise themselves to death. Those with Prader-Willi syndrome are unable to experience satiation. Night-eating syndrome and sleep eating disorders haunt evenings. Sufferers of gourmand syndrome are so elegant they prepare only the finest foods to not eat. Pica compels consumption, but not of food. Ruminators vomit up their food and reswallow it. Those with body dysmorphic disorder (dysmorphobia) cannot accurately recognize their true body shape. And we mustn't forget food avoidance emotional disorder, dysorexia, dysphagia, selective eating, pervasive refusal syndrome, pediatric autoimmune neuropsychiatric disorder associated with streptococcus (PANDAS) anorexia, anorexia mirabilis, and "holy anorexia."

Bulimia and binge eating disorder might be seen as the other two legs of the three-legged eating disorder stool in the corner on which parents suddenly find themselves. Anorexics restrict eating, bulimics eat in compulsive binges and then purge, and binge eaters eat in compulsive binges but do not purge. The categories are ragged and untidy: anorexics often purge, bulimics sometimes restrict, and binge eaters can purge and restrict. The common factor is this: emotional torture and the crippling of the ability to sustainably self-regulate normal consumption.

With a diagnosis of anorexia nervosa there is, however, a prognosis, and it is dismal. For those formally diagnosed, 20 percent will die in the following twenty years. Of the third who will be called "cured," 45 percent will never marry, they will likely be plagued by infertility, and their life expectancy may be reduced. The ones in the middle, who neither die nor are cured, live lives of furtive agony. Unlike "recovering" addicts and alcoholics, they can never abstain from the issue of eating. Several times a day every human must consume or not consume, measure or not measure, risk overdoing or undereating. Each bite is a decision. Every situation is a food or not-food crisis. Every friend is a potential betrayer of the secret. Every lover is conditional. Every family member is an enabler or left behind.

THERE IS A NAME, and there is a prognosis, but strangely there are no real answers.

I do not mean there are no counselors who will take on anorexic patients. There are eating disorder specialists, team approaches, in-patient clinics, therapeutic ranches, religious establishments—an entire industry waiting for your call. There are soothing books, websites, nonprofit educational foundations, and support groups. You can find online support, telephone consultations, spiritual counseling, seminars, and twelve-step programs.

But as you dive headlong into this informational maelstrom, hand and wallet outstretched, the lack of coherence will strike you. All those waiting to help really don't say exactly what causes anorexia. There is no "answer." For all that willingness out there to help, you will notice that no one is answering the most important question: if you don't know what causes anorexia, then how do you know how to treat it?

No one likes this question. When I ask it I am greeted with the wonderfully practiced therapeutic reflection: "What do you think?" But it is still a good question. And although the answers I got were vague, legalistic, unscientific, and defensive, I kept asking.

"Anorexia is about individuation, about finding a voice, about control," we were told. "Anorexia does not occur in a vacuum."

"Anorexia has no single cause" was another bone they threw us. It is meant to comfort but it did not. Instead we were left to imagine all the various ways we had failed, erred, looked away, spoken falsely, and generally been exposed as rotten parents. Were we at fault in many ways or really awful in one, we wondered. We stood willing to do, to accept, to change whatever we could to get our beloved, ebbing daughter back, but we were unclear about what the disease was, what caused it, and what on earth the cure was. I must have missed this class in school. I did get extra credit in Guilt 201 and honors in Angst for Mothers, so I knew the basic vocabulary. But this one seemed over my head.

It took us a long time, too long, before we realized that what the pile of popular books we bought and the pamphlets and the websites meant is that the cause of anorexia nervosa is not known. It is not known by the professionals who treat anorexics and it is not known by the researchers who study it. They don't know. There are a lot of theories, though—all of which you will feel very guilty about. And even as all the authorities admit they don't know what causes this deadly disease, they all agree on one thing: see a professional because they know what to do about it.

9

FOLKS, DON'T TRY THIS AT HOME!

WE WENT TO PROFESSIONALS to see what they do.

They see your child alone, and then you. This will not be explained in advance. If pressed, they will explain that they want to determine whether your child has anything to say that might point to abuse or coercion. If not pressed, they will expect you to wait your turn while they privately ask questions of your nearly mute and quite clearly delusional child. You will not know what your child is saying. You will not know what your child is hearing. You will suppress your tears in the waiting room and try not to stare at the even scarier-looking children in the tiny waiting room with their wretched, red-eyed parents.

The professional will listen to—and inexplicably believe—what your daughter tells him. He will note on the chart, as if based in reality, what she says she ate that day and for the past week. With any teenager this is an itty strategy. For an anorexic it is comically futile. Anorexics almost never believe they are anorexic. Anorexics almost always believe they take up more space than they do. Anorexics think saltines are fattening.

Asking a teenager the day of the week is unreliable. Asking anorexics how much they have eaten, or how they feel, or whether they have

conflicts with their mother is, well, silly. Anorexia is a disease charac-
terized by denial, irrationality, and alexithymia, which is the inability to
discern or describe one's emotions. Even I knew that. I had seen my share
of "very special" sit-com episodes. I had read a pamphlet or two. But
since my job was to sit in the waiting room and write a nonreimbursable
check before I left, I was not able to share my insights with the therapists. I was not asked.

I love my daughter; the sun rises and sets over her. But even before
anorexia rendered her temporarily mad in her fifteenth year, she would
not have remembered at what age she was toilet-trained or whether she
had birth trauma. I tried unsuccessfully to get her to remember her
Social Security number. I don't think she knew her own e-mail address.

But bring your daughter to a therapist for suspected anorexia and the
therapist will spend the billable hour listening to your sick child who has
been asked the same questions—under protest—by a succession of other
therapists. You will be expected to sign on with each new therapist who
has an opening in his or her weekly schedule. Second opinions are not
expected.

"So, we'll see you next week, same time."

But you are not used to hiring therapists. You are not used to being
peripheral to your child's welfare. You are willing to pay whatever it takes
to help your child, of course, but most of the questions are about insurance coverage. Your child's chart will end up including the following:
mistakes about her age and about her family background, wildly inac-
curate accounts of her eating habits, her feelings about her mother, and
a margin note on her mother's body size. These "facts" will become part
of her record. You will not be asked to confirm or document them,
because a fourteen-year-old's interpretation of the facts is sufficient.

In our case, there was not even a physical exam. (Except for weight.
They love their scales.)

If I bring my child for a measles shot, I have to sign a form confirm-
ing that I understand and accept the consequences of the vaccination
and will not hold legally responsible the administrator of the shot or the

physician's office or their heirs for any injury that results in the infinitesimally small chance of an untoward reaction. My daughter cannot get an abortion, birth control, a tattoo, or an ear piercing without my permission. They won't teach her the location of her uterus in health class without my signature. But I was sent to another room for evaluation after evaluation for an eating disorder that only I was insisting she had. I was asked few questions. I was told very little before or after.

"Privacy concerns."

I know the look that they give me when I protest. I am familiar with that "aren't you getting a little too involved?" gaze. I've been the "only one who complained," the only one to show up, and the only one to "ask these questions" before. I can take it. In the first few months of my daughter's anorexia my job was clear; secure a professional. He or she would know what to do. How to find one, how to judge their credentials and philosophy, and how to choose one was still something I needed to learn. I didn't know—and no one pointed out—any controversy on how to treat anorexia or lack of certainty about its causes. All I knew was that I was not going to give up, be economical, or just take "yes" for an answer.

I CREATED A DATABASE. It is the kind of thing I do. When I am job-seeking, I cross out all the jobs I don't want, then apply for the ones left unmarked. I do mazes by starting at all the dead ends and blocking them out until the only way through is all that remains. When I had to find a therapist for Olympia, I set out to first list all the possibilities, then rule the bad ones out. Then I would interview the remaining ones and make a choice.

That didn't work.

"See a professional" usually starts with the primary physician, in our case our daughter's pediatrician. I went, I cried through the appointment and then through what should have been the staff's lunch break, and I left with four therapists' names. Two were not taking new patients, one did not return my call, and one didn't take our insurance.

I called our community's health-care referral line and asked for mental health care providers in our county who treat eating disorders. It was the first time I said the words aloud to a stranger, but I was a good little Girl Scout parent, and I was going to get the best care I could. The two they gave me were not on my pediatrician's list, although we are all in the same small town.

I wrote down all the therapists in the yellow pages, downloaded the list of therapists within sixty miles from our insurance provider and checked several websites that gave referrals for eating disorder specialists. I added to my list every name that was mentioned by others on the list as they explained that they were not taking new patients or did not take our insurance or were no longer in practice.

The list grew longer, the live prospects shorter. I began looking in a larger radius from our home. I spoke personally to as many as I could and made appointments with the ones who had availability. Many, many, never called me back. A few called back long-distance and expressed their sympathy and gave advice, and their tone of grave sympathy only served to scare me more.

In the end, there were few choices. Appointments were difficult to get, and few could see us in the near future. It was impossible to ascertain what level of expertise we needed, or what experience a therapist or psychiatrist had with eating disorders. I struggled with discerning the difference between psychologists and psychiatrists and between counselors and therapists. I tried to decode the licensing and certifications and memberships. A good number of the therapists did not take clients under seventeen. Another few were blunt and said they did not feel comfortable working with anorexics at all, due to their physical instability.

Try living with one.

I'm picturing an interview with Ollie Oncologist.

"Oh, did you say your daughter has brain cancer? Oh. Well, I don't like to treat that kind of cancer. I mean, that is hard to treat. You have to open up the skull and all that. It's messy. I like breast cancer better. Do you have any breast cancer?"

Finding a professional was not working out like it was supposed to. The prescription often accepted as gospel in eating disorder literature is the "team approach." In the fantasy world of these manuals, the family doctor notices the problem during a routine checkup and sits the parent down for a difficult talk. The doctor then refers the grateful and contrite parent to a therapist nearby who has extensive experience with eating disorders. The therapist meets with the young person, then assembles a team that includes the physician, a dietician, a psychiatrist, and—if cooperative—the parents. In that Disneyland of Eating Disorder Treatment, the team meets regularly to discuss the patient and coordinate treatment. The team is very professional and well qualified to understand and guide the family and patient. Everyone agrees on the method and prognosis and treatment goals. Everyone looks forward to a full recovery and their invitations to be on educational panels entitled "Success Stories."

But I live in the real world. Here where I exist, the magic team approach happens in rare and blessed confluence, which was no place I could get to. In the real world, the doctor isn't comfortable with the topic and your anorexic does not want to be "treated" (perhaps it sounds too much like a dessert). In the real world, you have to choose a provider from your insurer's list, your child's coaches just want their star player to keep playing, your husband wants the kid to "snap out of it," your other kids are starting to act funny too, the therapists you consult don't tell you anything, and your anorexic is laughing at you.

Meanwhile, during diagnosis and assessment appointments, your anorexic—who is listening, not just providing data—is tutored in his or her craft:

"Do you purge?" they ask with both eyes on the questionnaire, pen poised.

"Do you stick your finger down your throat to make yourself vomit?"

"What is *your* ideal weight?"

"Do you use over-the-counter diet pills or diuretics?"

"Did you drink a lot of water before your weigh-in?"

"How many meals did you skip today? Only two? Is that all?"

Why not offer a primer? An anorexic gets so many of these questions and fills out so many questionnaires, you might as well just make a credit course out of it.

Meanwhile, although your anorexic is clearly growing more bizarre, no one examines her medically. None of the psychologists, psychiatrists, physical therapists, knee surgeons, coaches, or even our pediatrician ordered more than a perfunctory physical exam. No blood test or CAT scan. No one ruled out intestinal parasites, thyroid disease, a brain tumor, PANDAS, gallstones, chronic adrenal insufficiency, celiac disease, Addison's disease, diabetic gastroparesis, or any other of the kinds of illnesses misdiagnosed as anorexia that would have horrified me before, but at different points along the line all might have sounded like welcome diagnoses.

They just kept weighing her.

MY DAUGHTER WAS TREATED by way of her ears. A strange, one-way mirror of the senses. Asked things, told things. And as I watched her grow sicker it was clear to me—a mere mother—that she heard enough incoherence and madness around her that the insanity provided by her starving brain's cable service was no less trustworthy than the rest of us. The world was mad, and she was sane.

AN ANOREXIC RESISTS TREATMENT. It must be in the union contract somewhere. The belligerent and entrenched creature is forced to see a therapist, a nutritionist or two, and a trusted family doctor by parents who feel like they are transporting a caged and dangerous animal. The anorexic is given numerous—sometimes conflicting—instructions to "get better" from a disease that by this time seems like a friend and not an enemy. The anorexic believes he has no problem, that, in fact, he is finally in control of his life. He is in control and can stop—but why should he?—any time he wants.

Olympia humored me as we went from office to office. No matter what corner I thought I had logically wrestled her into, she escaped with a thin laugh: "I'm fine, Mom. You really ought to get some sleep. You seem stressed out."

ANOREXICS DON'T USUALLY get better through simple once-a-week therapy, but it is routinely the first thing tried. Outpatient therapy, if available nearby and covered by a family's insurance, is tried next. For some patients this brief loss of control and intensive self-inquiry is successful. For most it is not, and they either progress to hospitalization or they "age out" and go on to live an anorexic lifestyle as adults—where only life-threatening episodes will force them into care. Throughout, American parents are told to sit on their hands and keep their food to themselves.

In the hospital the anorexic is sometimes fed by nasal tube or intravenously until she is physically stable. She is then offered small incentives for finishing carefully calibrated amounts of calories; and punishments, such as not being allowed to call home, for failing to eat. Group and individual therapy then attempt to uncover the "underlying psychological and emotional issues." Upon release at a minimum "target weight" (which thereafter becomes the anorexic's maximum target weight), the sufferer goes home to starve up for the next round. Readmissions are considered routine.

Throughout this process your anorexic is told to discover "why." She is given a number of ideas to try on like fashionable jeans, such as "You have the classic signs of having hidden memories of sexual abuse. Who abused you?" or "You are afraid of growing up, aren't you?" Another tried-and-true classic is "You are not eating because it is the only thing you can control. Why don't you feel in control? Who is controlling you?"

And Mom and Dad's favorite, "You are freaking your parents out. Do you like that? You are speaking to your parents through not eating—why don't you just tell them how much you hate them? You do hate them, don't you? They've brought you here against your will, after all."

It is assumed that there is an answer to why your anorexic stops eating. Therapy is about finding that answer. You can volunteer one or they'll custom-fit one to suit.

Eventually, after therapy and the "normal" routine of repeated relapses, the anorexic redefines "recovery" as being alive. Differentiating the disease and the person is no longer attempted. As legal adulthood arrives, families drift apart in waves of blame, hope, more blame, and the inevitable spasms of recovery and regression. All are normal for anorexia.

OF COURSE, I DIDN'T KNOW all this as I was making my neat little database.

I knew that I knew nothing and had a lot to learn. I did not yet know that I was neither expected nor welcome to come to my own conclusions. All I knew for certain was that we had to get her well and get her back.

We would, wouldn't we?

10

THE ANOREXIA TABLE

To the world that fall, I think we appeared unchanged. We told a strict minimum number of people. We took in our paper every morning. We brought the kids to their calendar of activities. We did laundry and fed the dogs. But we did not answer the telephone. We made no invitations to dinner, and we were busy when invited. I begged off my volunteer commitments. I quit my part-time job. I stopped reading the book I ordered about college admissions, then I hid it from myself.

Olympia went to school and sat during "lunchtime" with what I sarcastically thought of as "the anorexia table." Her little friends had gone from frivolous to freakish in my mind's eye. Their similar hairstyles, exposed midriffs, miraculously low waistbands now seemed cruel and insidious. They were no longer silly girls passing through a brief phase, they were messengers of evil, purveyors of decay and early death. They were selling a sinewy seduction, they were sweeping her away.

Throughout her life I had intoned the postfeminist mantra of inner worth, individualism, body acceptance. I read from the playbooks parents like me use: the modern sensibility; the empowered electorate; the book-learned boomer belief in science and progress and *Parents* magazine Health Alerts. Refined sugar is bad, but let's not be obsessive. Provide educational toys and enriched environment. Disdain too much TV and unsupervised children. Always wear your seat belt and your helmet.

Olympia may look like the Popular Girl, but I always thought of that as a clever and disarming disguise. Her appearance belied the unique perspective within: she was what she appeared and much more. She learned of India from one grandfather, civil service from another. She had academia and the military, a barber, a convict, and a restaurateur in her family tree. She spoke Spanish and Chinese before she was three. This girl had traveled across the country and overseas and on airplanes alone. She visited relatives at the Parthenon and in Watts. She had milked goats, visited Disneyland with socialists, and started her own craft business for a season. I thought of her as a stealth bomb of unique knowledge poised to change the world. She had insights I could never have, access like few of her peers, assets that meant something. Her palette of colors went beyond skin deep, she was empathetic, and athletic, engaged, informed, and as stern in principles as she was well-versed in nail enamels. I genuinely liked her, admired her, and was her biggest fan.

But still her *Seventeen* magazines rankled me. The drawings of pretty faces, collages of pop stars, the attraction to cheerleading. I never expected to have to make it clear what I didn't approve of. I liked it better when I was decorating her life with all the good and wholesome things I could bring her and she went along with my worldview.

Long before the anorexia hit, my lectures and parade of role models skated off her consciousness. They were not rejected as much as they had no traction. This annoyed me but did not scare me. I was, frankly, growing tired of arguing these issues. I wondered if it was all just part of her growing up—or of my growing old. Besides, I was growing frumpy and fat and trying hard to accept that gracefully. I was not yet doing the purple clothing thing, but I had begun to look forward to the well-deserved cronish irritability that I expected to earn in the near future. I remember being annoying to my mother as she peeled off to a life in which she was her own center. Perhaps it was natural that my daughter would not embrace the same values and politics that I did. I thought that pressing too hard might turn her further away, so I backed off, when I could resist, from criticizing a lifestyle full of clothes and thinness and appearances.

MY FINAL SILENT COMPLICITY came over my shoulder in the car. Three freshmen sat in the back seat, and I stayed quiet as one does when allowed to overhear the conversation of one's moral elders.

"I'm going to have to go on a diet to get into my bathing suit." This from the most ectomorphic of the three.

"Me, too!" the second one chirped as though this were the most practiced conversation in their songbook.

"I'm so fat!" the first one said.

My daughter said nothing. She returned my pained expression with resignation. "I told you so," her face said.

I was too shocked to respond, then or later, to my eternal regret. For the first time I really saw the world she lived in and wanted to live in. Where girls in the middle of puberty hated the bodies they also felt compelled to flaunt. Where the thinnest girl wins by saying that she is fat.

I heard in that conversation and saw in my daughter's eyes that nothing I said seemed rational. A lifetime of role models and life experiences and a family that, nearly as much as is possible, thought of appearance as nothing more than another small asset—all meant nothing to her. My influence seemed bankrupt. And I think she hated me just a little for that. I think she wondered who was abandoning whom.

11

SHOW ME THE MONEY

WE WOULD HAVE PAID anything we had to cure her. In the first few months we drained our bank account without regard to our future. Saving her was our future. College and retirement were frivolous notions. I made many, many appointments. I did not ask prospective therapists or doctors what they charged. I wrote the check at the end of each session without knowing whether our insurance would pick any of it up. Samuel and I didn't care. We were terrified. We were naïve.

"This has got to be what having money is for," Samuel said, and he concentrated on making more. Then I spent it, without restraint, on anything involving food, therapy, books, research papers, long-distance bills, keeping Elijah calm, and pretending that everything was all right and would be all right. It takes time to adjust yourself to the new truth that your old life is over and a new one has begun. First, you just spend money.

Families mortgage homes, declare bankruptcy, and give up custody of their children in order to get treatment after their cash runs out. Insurance companies will not tell you what they will cover beforehand. One mother I know finally got her daughter into a program that was

helping, but the insurance company only approved ten days at a time—
with no assurance that it would be renewed. Imagine living in hope and
hell in ten-day increments, over and over. Mental health services are
often limited and anorexia lives on a strange fault line between "medical" and "mental." People find their claims for therapy denied because
anorexia is a medical condition, but after stabilization (defined as reach-
ing a certain weight), their claims are denied because anorexia is a psychological condition, not medical. On the psychiatric ward they often
can't treat the physical issues of the eating disorder. In the medical wing
they don't address the psychological issues of the eating disorder.

Current treatment of anorexia costs more than $30,000 per year of
life saved. What happens to those who don't have insurance or cash?
What happens to those who cannot send their child or loved one or
themselves to a ranch for art therapy for months? Families find themselves at the mercy of emergency room doctors and social workers. Each
crisis brings a new set of providers, each time the families start over.

Psychiatric hospital wards, repeatedly. Alcoholism, frequently. Suicide, too often. Families drained of resources, more often than you
know, because no one is going to talk about it. Families confronting
anorexia live in secret, in fear, in a private hell of uncertainty, guilt, and
hopelessness. Their child rarely wants help. The parents are profoundly
alone. Marriages are strained. Other siblings smolder and resent.

If anorexia were only a concern for the rich and beautiful, I guess we
could stifle our schadenfreude. If it were only the concern of this mother,
who obviously fits the profile of an overinvolved, obsessive suburban
mother on a rampage, OK, so be it. But what if it can strike anyone,
regardless of their ability to pay?

Trust me, no parents in our position think it will happen to them.
But it can. Anorexia's expense is counted in lives destroyed, marriages
upended, siblings estranged, friendships rethought, jobs lost, and dollars spent. You would pay anything to save your child, but to whom, and
for what?

12

NOT EATING WITH YOUR ANOREXIC

OLYMPIA STARTED TENTH GRADE wearing a new outfit. Of course she needed new clothes for the new school year, but we also knew that her body had changed. Those hateful little new clothes meant that her monthlong starvation now inhabited her wardrobe; regaining the weight would mean going back to the old clothes. Getting better, which we still thought of as something that might just spontaneously happen, could not happen without her noticing—to a fashion-conscious fourteen-year-old, clothes were too tangible a thing. Unlike many anorexics, she wasn't interested in baggy clothes and concealing layers. The low-cut jeans and tight-fitting shirts were like a boa constrictor of anorexia cinching its measure around her proportions.

Her grandmother and I actually hatched a plot where we would go back and buy duplicates of everything she just bought, in successively larger sizes, to replace the miniatures as she regained her health. "The labels," Dina sighed.

"Oh, the labels," I agreed.

She'd read the labels. We knew she would. Too bad. It was a good idea.

I should explain that we bought into what we heard: don't argue with her. I said this to many people, therapists and others, as a sign that I was responding correctly, and they all nodded sagely. We treated this person who used to be our daughter with live-grenade tenderness: we didn't want her to get worse. It was emotional extortion, a hostage-taking crisis: she had the gun to her head and threatened to use it if we tried to take it away. OK, keep the gun, just don't shoot it. But wouldn't you like a cookie?

We tried heroically, out on the ledge, to talk her out of it. We counted up her calories, cited statistics, mentioned hospitals where people went when they became very ill. We thought she was willful, defiant, even making this up. We thought she misunderstood something, made a logical error. We thought she was trying to make us crazy. Here, clearly, was the teenage rebellion we had heard so much about.

Eventually, I called one set of my parents because I just needed to hear their voices. Samuel and I had agreed early on not to tell anyone, and no one seemed to notice that our very nice little lives had derailed. My parents lived nowhere near us, but I needed to make my confession and receive my penance. I described the dead eyes, the bony shoulders, the cold skin with all the horror and shame of a failing parent to her own parents. The month since we had seen them on vacation seemed a long time ago. It was, actually—ninety-nine meals had passed. Bewildered, they comforted me with universal platitudes and joined the circling of the wagons. "Maybe she just needs to see how bad it is, maybe that will change her mind."

We all believed in her mind. That she had changed it and could change it back. I read about anorexia being about "control" and "individuation." I believed it. I believed everything I read and heard and remembered. I swallowed it all.

Meanwhile, we sat in baited horror watching her eat and not eat, decide and not decide, fight us and then beg us for help she refused to take. She was confused and frightened and happy and anxious in alternate moments. We watched, and we bit our tongues instead of our suppers.

WE DIDN'T HIRE the first two therapists. They seemed to treat Olympia as though she were rational. They each explained to me kindly that they had experience with these things and that they would talk with Olympia about body issues and media images and growing up. I knew Olympia saw through them. *I* saw through them. I wanted someone to take a harder line, to be more assertive with her. If I couldn't talk her out of this then I needed someone stronger than me.

What I liked first about Joy the Licensed Professional Counselor was that she answered her own phone. She sounded authoritative and knowledgeable. She wasn't particularly nice, which was perfect. She said things in our first conversation that I had been hoping someone would say, like that Olympia could recover and that Joy would assemble a team of professionals to support her. On the center's website I saw listings for parent support groups and eating disorder support groups. And she could give us an appointment the very next week.

Every day before that first appointment was another three meals to not eat. We started going to restaurants, thinking the choices would make it more attractive. We would offer Olympia food with a smile, then suffer with another smile as she refused. But we did not fight her. We understood that that would only make things worse. We went on with life as if it was normal, at least when she was around. She went to school. Our son, Elijah, went to preschool. Samuel went to work. And I went into a frenzy of telephone calls, reading, and crying.

Olympia had an appointment with Joy every Wednesday evening at seven. She forgot about the appointment every week until I told her it was time to go. One week she would say she didn't see the point, the next she would say "good" in such a way that implied I was going to be told on. Every week she was quieter afterward, stiffer. We drove her there, an hour away, with immense relief: we were doing something. Eight weeks went by in this way, and Olympia ate only enough to keep herself walking. We didn't argue. She was getting therapy, and everything was going to be OK.

"Joy says I shouldn't do this."

"Joy says it is all right for me to do that."

Welcome to the world of co-parenting with your child's therapist. Welcome to the world of triangulation, marginalization, and implicit guilt. The two of them had their private meetings, we got a bill, and Olympia got worse. We were "doing all we should," Joy said when I begged for more guidance, but what we were doing was nothing. Just a daily charade at being the us we were before. Except now we had no active part in it. And no authority. Joy was the authority.

Olympia did not talk much about the sessions. Some things surfaced nonetheless. She mentioned that Joy had anorexia, that Joy's daughters had eating disorders, that Joy had suffered childhood abuse, that Joy's husband had recently died. We learned these things from Olympia's tantalizingly off-handed statements over time—as if they would not shock us, as if we had no right to be shocked. We had sent her, after all. Joy said almost nothing to us. The meetings she originally promised never materialized. There was a word or two when she came out to get Olympia. A few conversations on the phone at my request. Joy said she was speaking with the "team" but no one talked to us.

Olympia had exactly 167 hours and ten minutes a week outside of Joy's office. Fifty minutes within.

There were things that scared me about the whole business at the time. I felt anxious in the tiny waiting room. There was no receptionist, only a panel of buttons to push to tell your therapist behind the self-locking doors that you had arrived. What I pictured as a comforting center of coordinated and smooth services seemed more like a New Age rented-by-the-hour massage center.

The teenage anorexia support group would often be waiting their turn when the adult overeating support group was leaving. Picture that. I needed therapy after watching the two constituencies squeeze past each other in the narrow room. The overeaters, you understand, were laughing.

The other waiting parents preferred not to speak with each other. I think the wild, zealous look in my eyes scared them off. We all whispered in the small space, clearly audible nonetheless, but the effort was appreciated. We all tried to seem smaller, quieter, not there: anorexia parentica.

Before the scheduled surgery to repair her knee, the surgeon asked for a routine pre-admission blood test. The nurse could not get a vein. Olympia was so dehydrated her normally athletic veins wouldn't rise. It took four tries. Olympia began to cry, a weak, inarticulate sort of cry with no tears. More like whimpering. She let me hold her hand and I said "I'm here," but I felt as if I were alone. Olympia looked ill and, even worse, she spoke without affect.

The surgeon cancelled the surgery indefinitely. Anesthesia was too dangerous.

Sometimes I asked Olympia whether the therapy was going well. I wasn't supposed to ask about the specifics, but after weeks of meetings I had no idea where things were going. She said it was "OK." One day we were pretending to eat and I timidly asked whether she and Joy had discussed whether she should start eating more.

"We don't talk about food."

13

WAIVERING

"Am I supposed to tell her everything? Like, anything about us and myself?"

Olympia had never been entrusted to another adult outside our family. She is a private person and has never shown an interest in being very confessional with her friends. She doesn't seek the spotlight and is reserved, observant, and respectful. Now she was sitting with this adult she didn't know, talking about personal issues. And we made her do it.

"Oh, yes!" I gushed. "You are completely safe with Joy. Everything you say is private and the only rule is that you should be completely honest with her and yourself. There are no secrets or things too private in this family that you cannot share."

I believed this strongly. I had seen therapists in the past. I valued the therapeutic relationship and the benefits of impartial counseling. But I don't think I misread a look of disappointment in Olympia's eyes. Perhaps even contempt. I believe, in some way, she felt betrayed to be turned loose like this.

Joy took our daughter as a patient, and since I had never considered having my child in such a relationship, I had not planned my role as parent in the equation. I went into it assuming that there was An Answer, that the therapist would Know It and share It with Us, and that we'd all work on It Together. I was desperate for help and quite clueless on the disease, its causes, and the therapeutic methodology.

When I called Joy looking for an appointment I was looking for an ally, an expert, a consultant. I was not seeking a parental surrogate or planning to turn our parental authority over to another person. As with medical consultation, I saw myself and my husband as partners and supporters in the group effort of helping Olympia help herself. We were not looking for a way out; quite the contrary, we were looking for the way in.

It took me a while to figure out that that was not the game Joy played. She treated Olympia as she would any patient, like an autonomous adult. Their conversations were confidential, and the therapist's responsibility was to be the center of a wheel of communication of which we, the parents, were the least important spokes. I did not know what transpired in her conversations with our physician or with the nutritionist. I signed a waiver to allow them all to converse; in so doing, I put myself, without understanding it, out of the loop.

When I asked, having some research and vocabulary under my own belt, what therapeutic approach she subscribed to, Joy answered mysteriously, "Eclectic." However, this was not helpful, even after I looked it up, along with other good vocabulary words like "enmeshment" and "countertransference."

There were more smoke and mirrors when I attended a parent's informational meeting at the center one night and was admonished beforehand that everything shared in that room was confidential. We all nodded sincerely. The collective weight of anguish and confusion in the room bound us like a cult.

We were given a handout and asked to read aloud from it in turns around the circle. The sheet told us that our children's eating disorders were the result of "deep emotional issues" in a family. One mother started to cry.

I spoke up and asked about all I had been reading about genetic causes and new research.

I was stared down by the group leader. She sighed and went on taking confessions from the other parents. I felt like a wife recently moved to Stepford.

The next morning I called Joy with alarm, suddenly suspicious of what Olympia was being taught at the center.

"Yes, I heard what you said last night."

"Not that I have any secrets, Joy, but wasn't that a confidential meeting?"

"Well, we didn't mean between the professionals."

THE REST OF THAT DAY I fumed.

The next morning, I dialed.

I worried a bit that I would be in trouble with Joy, but I called a large teaching hospital two hours away and asked to speak to their Eating Disorder Clinic. I was hoping for some advice or a referral to another therapist. I scheduled an evaluation, knowing they were the biggest and most reputable clinic near us. I had given up on finding a local psychiatrist. Of the two Joy suggested, one didn't take fourteen-year-olds and one was no longer practicing. The clinic made the appointment as if they did it every day.

I confided in an acquaintance whose daughter had dropped out of school with binge eating disorder. She said, "I don't want to scare you, but you should be prepared to check her in."

14

BRING IN THE CLOWNS

Booking a Stay with Ronald McDonald

LIFE AS WE KNEW IT was over. We were refugees and Olympia and I had both been crying. So it made no sense that we were laughing in the hospital cafeteria.

But even when you have just become an "Against Medical Advice" scofflaw and your next step seems to be into an abyss, hospital cafeteria food is still a hard sell. The desiccated meats and limp, soggy breads displayed before us would not appeal to anyone. But we burst into laughter at the absurdity of the moment. We laughed because it was lunchtime and Olympia was anorexic, because her EKG had been just good enough to avoid forced admittance and we couldn't get Samuel on the telephone, and because here in a cafeteria full of hospital workers and visitors, Olympia was turning up her nose at the sandwiches.

For a moment we were both absolutely in the same reality, and it was laughable. The two of us were strangers in a strange world—but we were together. Of course she would turn down the food, any food. And the food really did look awful—I was not able to pretend it did not. We had no idea what to do when we drove away from the hospital. It was funny because, as usual, I would have eaten whatever was available. And because once upon a time Olympia would have loved a place like this— a new place to eat and to people-watch.

In frustration I had demanded that Olympia just pick up a sandwich, and she looked at me as if I were crazy. And we both laughed. Because we were both crazy, and, for an instant at least, we both knew it.

THERE WERE SO MANY funny things.

It was funny that the eating disorder clinic at the hospital was a crowded, overstuffed hallway with no windows. Why have all the places we have waited for eating disorder specialists been confined, overfilled places?

It was funny how the whole procedure seemed more like a clandestine abortion than the state-of-the-art workup I expected. The payment was large, by check, and due in advance. Her eating disorder record, being psychiatric, was filed separately from her "medical" record at the hospital, so the insurance company didn't have access to it and I couldn't order a copy of it through the main hospital in which it sat.

The two of us filled out clipboard questionnaires for fifteen minutes, and then a doctor, whose qualifications I was not given, took Olympia off into another area of offices for almost an hour. Then she came back to get me, and we switched. Once seated I was told without preamble that my daughter needed to be left "today" at the hospital for six weeks, during which we could visit her on weekends. The following six weeks we would be expected to live with her at a nearby Ronald McDonald House, while she graduated to day-patient status, as our home was too far away to commute.

"She's fourteen," I said, feebly.

Therapeutic silence.

"No," I said, in more words but with no more meaning.

Therapeutic irritation.

"Thank you," I added.

That was funny—I said thank you.

I also said no. In retrospect, that was even funnier.

IT WAS REALLY FUNNY that anyone would think of asking me to turn my fourteen-year-old child over to strangers in a hospital on the strength of a fifty-minute consultation with that child, without consulting any other professional, her medical records, or even her parents. That they would want to instantly end school, friendships, family life. Before calling me in, the doctor told Olympia the plan—then left her terrified and alone in the hallway while they broke the news to me. I guess they only had space in the office for one crying female at a time.

"You told her this?" I asked the doctor, incredulous that such a thing would be done without my knowledge or consent.

She had.

Nothing about the program was explained. I'd get better communication from someone about to pierce my daughter's ears than I was offered by these strangers in their messy cavern. They only told me that my kid is really sick, leave her here, and go home. It wasn't that I didn't think she was sick; I knew that. It wasn't that I didn't want help; I did. It was the all-or-nothing, we'll-take-over-from-here attitude. It was a dead stop to all that had come before—school, family life, parenting—and I, her mother, was not needed.

What is left after such a thing as dropping your fourteen-year-old off against her will to the care of strangers? What disease makes a family so expendable? Anorexia.

IT WAS FUNNY HOW the doctor seemed to need to hurry things up and how disinterested she was in my gravely ill daughter as soon as I turned down her hospitality.

But the funniest thing was, the clinic needed us more than we needed it.

There are many clinics and ranches and centers for recovery, refeed-ing, and retreat. The websites are in lavender and show impossibly healthy women (and one token man) caught in the middle of grateful and delighted smiles. The brochures promise personalized treatment, multidisciplinary approaches, and comforting surroundings. None dis-cuss the quality of their food service. Otherwise they might sound too much like spa vacations. Price, as in any exclusive club, is only available by telephone consultation. Spas, however, are usually cheaper.

You can have your child (if he is a minor) admitted to a psych ward against his will to be stabilized or to an eating disorder unit (if he is an adult) in which a minimum weight will be determined for discharge. You can do inpatient, outpatient, stepped-up levels, intensive, or half-day programs. But you usually cannot do this anywhere near where you live. These programs, though not rare, are widely dispersed. You will have few choices.

Your child can check herself out, in many cases, or be thrown out for lack of cooperation. The clinics won't keep her long enough to cure her, and they cannot tell you in advance how long a stay your insurance will cover. Your child, minor or technically adult, will be discharged to your formerly incompetent and counterproductive hands with the expecta-tion that readmission is "a normal part of recovery."

I discovered the world of eating disorders has two speeds: 0 and 120. You can get indefinite and indifferent care from eating disorder thera-pists and nutritionists who follow the old school in weekly sessions, or you can get top-of-the-line hospitalization and monitoring in isolation from your family and your life. It is the story of mental health care in our times.

15

"THE WISHES OF A.N."

"Bring her home," Samuel said.

"I'm bringing her home," I choked.

It was the worst day of my life. And probably of Olympia's and Samuel's as well. I made very hollow, very short phone calls to those who had to be told. Yes, she is that sick, and no, we did not admit her.

My mother's first response was "Why?" I forgive her.

It sounded foolish, I guess, to defy the professionals. Dangerous. Reckless and arrogant. Who were we to think we knew better than highly trained professionals? Yet it was inconceivable to institutionalize Olympia. It wasn't that we knew what to do; it was that we just knew that sending her away wasn't going to happen. She wasn't moving away, not without us.

We had read what to expect in a hospital. Until we could figure out what else to do, we decided to do ourselves what hospitals do. The first thing was that she was going to eat. If the hospital would measure and serve her meals and watch her eat, then so would we. If the hospital staff would stay with her after meals to keep her from purging, so would we. If the hospital would restrict her exercise, so would we. No arguing, no negotiation. To avoid the hospital, we became the hospital. I refused to believe that the thing she needed least was us.

It was never said directly, but in the storm of emotion and the piece-work of "normal" left to us, we were establishing an entirely new relationship.

It was a crazy notion, even to us: do not listen to your own mind, to the shards of your intellect, to what you think the world is whispering in your ear. Listen to us, and us alone. Trust us. We are your parents. We know what we are doing. Follow our directions. And she did.

She didn't appear to, of course. To the untrained eye, she appeared to hate us. She searched for the cruelest things to say. She bargained and then howled. There was rage, derision, physical pain, comparisons to dictators and legendarily abusive parents of our acquaintance. But the most insidious was the impossibility of distinguishing that blank glacial stare from the normal adolescent bargaining and blather one expects and vaguely remembers reading about in the warranty booklet.

Yet, here was the difference: it all had to do with food. That realization—that it was the disease that was fighting us, not her—made it possible for us not to blame her. We externalized the illness. As heartrending as it was, we had to forget and disregard the person we up to that moment knew, loved, and trusted. We did not know if she would ever be back, but it was clear that our Olympia was gone and the fight to save her meant living with this stranger we neither knew nor liked.

The funny thing was, the person I most longed to talk to, to share the story of this bizarre twist in our lives, was her. I missed her as if she were away. As if I were involuntarily participating in a cosmic exchange student program wherein I had to house, clothe, and feed this impostor for some while to get my child back.

My "Twilight Zone" daughter enjoyed her accommodations. She delighted in the outward appearance of our family as normal. She took my daughter's babysitting jobs and messed up her room. She took her classes and made straight As, knowing that would trouble us with its macabre normality in what was really an abnormal time. She retained my daughter's friends, learned their secrets, and—I'm sure this particularly delighted her—they never knew. She had that on us—that we had agreed to keep this knowledge private to protect her reputation and future. Her school and our neighbors never knew, only a few of our friends. We were willing and able to cross that line, but it stood as a mutually respected Rubicon. The charade defined our conduct. There was a vague sense that what we were doing was clandestine, mildly criminal. It was a quiet, invisible siege.

It was clear that Olympia could not eat without help, and it was clear that we were not going to let her starve. Beyond that we knew little.

In exchange for the privacy outside our home, the rules inside became a cocoon of ritual. We reinvented parenting. We cobbled together a program based on medical journal accounts, overheard concepts, old-fashioned authoritarian parenting channeled through our grandparents, and, always, the fear of the alternative. For her, that fear was hospitalization; for us, it was her death.

It turned out that we were not alone.

Samuel, who was more efficient than I on the Internet, sent me a link to an article (*Spoonfeeding Anorexics* by Carrie Golus) that changed everything. The description of a family-based treatment for adolescent anorexics said something I really needed to hear:

For anorexics, eating is an ordeal: patients obsessively calculate and recalculate calories or refuse to eat unless food is arranged in a certain pattern. Parents can end this obsession by temporarily revoking their daughter's responsibility for choosing to eat. When she begins to gain weight she regains her ability to make healthy choices because, [Dr. Daniel] Le Grange says, "obsessive thoughts and feelings are side effects of the starvation."

Shocking. Revolutionary. Parents could be good for their kids. No one we'd consulted and nothing we'd read was saying anything like this. I rushed out to purchase literature about these new ideas.

Dr. James Lock, in *Treatment Manual for Anorexia Nervosa*, said, "They should nourish the patient according to their profound state of malnutrition, not according to the wishes of A.N."

The wishes of A.N. My daughter had been listening to the wishes of her disease, that malignant alien voice in her head. But it turned out that I didn't have to listen too.

These radical ideas are known informally as the Maudsley approach, named after the London hospital in which the approach was first researched. Although it had been used since the 1980s in England, with higher success rates than any other known therapy for adolescent anorexia, the few articles about it in the American press called it "controversial."

We now knew what to call ourselves: Maudsleyans! It is a wonder I didn't immediately begin using a British accent and emigrate. Now we knew there was something out there—a method, an approach, an alternative way of thinking. Samuel and I knew immediately we were on to something, something that did not automatically blame parents or assume sexual abuse. An approach that said eating was the first line of action and not a cruel thing to make your child do.

For the first time since Olympia stopped eating normally, I felt the raw, blind fear lift and saw a glimpse of a plan.

I WAS NOT IMMEDIATELY critical of the orthodoxy of eating disorder treatment, which treats the illness by taking you off to talk you out of it and hoping to weigh you into submission. I went into it prepared to find the best and the most aggressive treatment and to follow every order to the letter. I did not set out to run the show. I did my research so I could best support the system that exists. But I drew the line at abandoning my child. And the description of the Maudsley approach turned so much of the gospel of eating disorder treatment on its head, it started to sound like the real world again.

". . . treat the illness like any other illness."

"Food is seen as medicine."

"Puts the family directly in charge of making the patient eat."

Programs at Stanford, Columbia University, the University of Chicago, and the University of Pittsburgh are now listening, too.

I tried to find a therapist who subscribed to the Maudsley approach, now that I had a name for it. I contacted people in London and at Stanford; I re-called the therapists in our area, trying to get referrals. I went to Joy and asked her to work with our whole family in this approach.

IN THAT FINAL MEETING with Joy—the one in which she fired us and then, in a baby voice, told Olympia "I'm going to *miss* you!"—my husband asked Joy why she had not wanted to work with us as a family or encourage us to feed Olympia.

"It takes a long time to determine whether these girls have suffered abuse."

Nine more pounds, I thought. Olympia lost another nine pounds and all those days of her health while she went to weekly therapy with someone who suspected us of abusing her.

Samuel, in particular, took this hard. "She thinks I abused my daughter."

I didn't say anything, but I couldn't help thinking, "Maybe they all do."

WE DROVE HOME from the appointment silently bewildered. We arrived late to pick up Elijah at a friend's house. The tension was probably obvious. The story was that we had been at Olympia's "doctor" appointment—everyone knew about her knee. The couple looked at us and then her.

"Well," said the husband, taking a stab at the quiet, "Olympia, your knee may be broken but you look great! Never better. Doesn't she look great?"

In my mind I killed him. In my mind I murdered that poor kind man there in front of his small children and equally kind wife. Violent, spattering, instant. He didn't deserve it. He was a nice guy. But in my mind, boom. In Samuel's mind I think the guy went down hand to hand with a broken neck. But I definitely had a gun.

Olympia didn't need an imaginary weapon, however. Her smile was lethal.

"Thank you," she said. "I'm feeling better."

As we drove home, we realized we had been fired. We were on our own.

16

A FAMILIAR ODOR

To UNDERSTAND HOW RADICAL an approach Maudsley is, you must understand the history of anorexia treatment. From 1978, when the universally cited book, *The Golden Cage*, by Hilde Bruch, M.D., was published, it was received wisdom that the phenomenon of self-starving in young girls is a manifestation of deep inner anguish, expressed through their control of eating. Bruch described a disease that "selectively befalls the young, rich, and beautiful," which was rapidly increasing and indicative of an "overcompliant" child who has "been deprived by her parents of the right to live her own life."

The book is still in print and available in bookstores; it was one of the first I purchased in my search for anorexia information. It was a convenient first introduction because it confirmed all my worst fears: that our negligence or our actions had set up and triggered our daughter's illness, that we were the worst thing for her. Bruch maintained:

The development of anorexia nervosa is so closely related to abnormal patterns of family interaction that successful treatment must always involve resolution of the underlying family problems, which may not be identifi-

able as open conflicts; on the contrary, quite often excessive closeness and
overintense involvements lie at the roots. . . . All anorexics are involved with
their families in such a way that they have failed to achieve a sense of
independence.

I had no trouble seeing this as our family's problem. These were not
new criticisms, this described us! People have often remarked on how
close Olympia and I are and how she is "so mature" and comfortable
around adults. She has been known to speak to us in public—even with
a peer nearby. Once again, what had seemed before the illness to be an
asset, a source of joy, was suddenly suspect. Was her former happiness a
sign of dysfunction? Was our family closeness really a bad thing?

The next two books I read were first-person accounts of anorexia
survivors that chronicled how overbearing mothers on hypocritical diets
sent their sensitive daughters into entirely justified suffering, even near
death, but who each one day took control of her destiny and got better.
Perfect! Let the self-loathing begin.

A succession of self-help and everything-you-need-to-know books
followed. A pattern emerged: anorexia is a response to the world, a way
of controlling a life that is intolerable. Anorexia is a cry for help from
your child, who is overwhelmed by media images, societal pressures, and
early sexuality. Your anorexic has probably been sexually abused, and if
you don't believe that then you must be in denial. You, as parent, while
perhaps not strictly at fault, did not protect your child from these influ-
ences. You must face up to the responsibility of changing the negative
patterns and choices you have made with your child—or get out of the
way while your kid and her therapist clean up your mess.

The most brilliant marketing strategist could not have designed a
more perfectly targeted message to a more receptive audience. Parental
guilt, evil media, stressful society, sex! Who could argue? Let's put the
therapist on automatic withdrawal at our bank; this is going to take a
while.

The whole toxic family explanation, however, had a familiar odor. It didn't take me long to figure out why. Five years before my family's entry into the world of extreme psychiatry, I learned of a nonblood relative who suffers from paranoid schizophrenia. Frightened for her relatives and their genetic inheritance, I spent a very painful month of reading and researching. I evolved, during that period, from what I think was a popular misconception of mental illness to a new understanding of the makeup of consciousness and sanity. Before I did this exploration I thought of schizophrenics and the mentally ill, when I bothered to think of them at all, as pitiful and weak-willed people. I saw their disease as sad, but something you could pull up your socks and be stronger than. I used the word "crazy" as if it were either pitiable or embarrassing, but not involuntary.

I learned how schizophrenia was, until painfully recent history, believed to be caused by overprotective mothering. Somehow the idea never occurred to people that the bizarre delusions of a child might cause alarm—and that their mothers might end up appearing pretty frazzled. We look back on those dark ages of psychiatry with forgiveness and a bit of patronizing, and we no longer buy the "schizophrenogenic mother" theory of the 1940s or the Freudian view of schizophrenia as repressed homosexuality. Schizophrenia is now understood to be an organic brain disorder, one whose ravages can be discerned in sophisticated brain imaging. It is treatable, though not cured, by increasingly refined drugs and is no longer blamed on caregivers, who bore the suffering of their loved ones and their own guilt simultaneously.

The parents of autistic children might also recognize the odor I was getting from the anorexia explanations. A disease that was only discretely diagnosed in 1943, autism affects one out of 250 births. The Freudian belief that "refrigerator mothers" were at fault sent these children to foster homes and lingers on in the antagonism and mistrust between parents of autistic children and the psychiatric profession. Now that autism, although not completely understood, is known to be a medical condition, autistic children are diagnosed and treated earlier and more effectively. Time is no longer wasted on blaming the parents.

If schizophrenia and autism were once, in the absence of a medical test to diagnose them, seen as caused by the people around them, I began to wonder if anorexia couldn't be similarly misunderstood. I thought about other diseases, like multiple sclerosis and heart disease, that are often misdiagnosed as "only" psychological. It doesn't help that anorexia nervosa is considered a female disease. There are nine female victims for every male, apparently, although diagnosing bias may undercount them. The fact that it is believed to be a girl thing to diet and a girl thing to get eating disorders may have trivialized both treatment and public information. As the leading cause of early death in girls, one wonders why something so historically deadly could be perceived as vanity or as self-expression.

I think if they were walking into lakes we'd find energy to look a bit deeper. Ophelia, in our age, would be on Paxil and deconstructing the Prince of Denmark in a group session over frappuccinos.

It doesn't take a raving feminist to wonder whether the attention paid to and the politics of eating disorders may be less than entirely evidence-based. Too many constituencies seem to like this disease, even relish it. Feminist literature blames patriarchy. Fundamentalists blame licentious culture. Family advocates blame the lack of family dinners. Child advocates blame grabby parents. Freudians find symbols. I have not found it yet, but I'm pretty sure there's a vegetarian lobby blaming meat-eaters and a beef board pointing the finger at vegans.

I looked again for data on physical causes. I was looking for misdiagnoses, of course, but even more for scientists publishing data that support the idea that anorexia is the body's assault on the mind, rather than the other way around. There is plenty. I gathered a basketful. I carried it with me to eating disorder specialists who patted me on the back and tried to placate me with "chicken and egg" analogies.

Sometimes they admitted that they just don't know.

"That stuff all looks the same to me," said one.

"It isn't important what causes it," said another.

"It is like an elephant," the smartest one admitted. "We all see only the part we're trained to understand."

17

SNAKE SWALLOWS SELF

I HATE THE DIET INDUSTRY. I hate the ads that promise "Lose all the weight you want" and "Lose inches" and "Money-back guarantee." I always disliked them for their tackiness, their greed, and their smug understanding that although the pills and programs did not work you would be back.

I hate how people are always talking about their diets and vacillating over éclairs. I wish I could take back every "diet" I have heard of or went on, and incinerate them in a bonfire of my vanities. I know there is a difference between overeating and undereating and the necessity of finding a lifestyle that works for each individual, and I myself will never again be able to eat as I please. But knowing what I do now, diets make me want to cry.

The words, "I lost five pounds in one week" sounds entirely different to the parent of an anorexic.

I do, however, love to use the diet industry against itself.

None of the literature I found on the Maudsley approach was specific about how the family should eat with their anorexic, only that it

must be done. The family has permission to do it, and we took that permission with gratitude and a passion. But there was no manual to help
you plan meals or present them nor guidelines to map out your short-
and long-term goals. So, living in a culture saturated by dieting information that now seemed backward and disordered, we simply trans-
posed the numbers. To refeed our emaciated child we used the world of
low-cal, low-carb, label-consciousness, and energy-balancing to our own
devices. Although I never did blame the diet cartel for my daughter's illness, we did use them to get her back.

I BOUGHT A COMPUTER PROGRAM called DietPower, which not only
counted calories, but also fat grams, water intake, and twenty-one or so
nutrients. It graphed current weight and metabolism and showed over
time what your projected weight would be. The program could not, however, compute why I kept inputting extra calories: "Alert: You have
recorded 3,492 calories today; at projected rates you will gain five pounds
over your target weight." Exactly.

For four strange months, I calibrated and recalculated, inputted and
schemed. Samuel was our chef and created elaborate multicourse meals
with amazing calorie counts. Adding whipped cream to everything put
us closer to the weekly goal of Olympia gaining two to three pounds. A
Big Mac put us ahead by a meal. Stock in Krispy Kreme shot up. Samuel's greatest triumph was a milkshake that contained 1,750 calories per
serving. I had to applaud. He had to bow.

The program gave a satisfying daily, weekly, monthly, and quarterly
report. I became so precise and focused on the program that I looked
forward to finishing dinner so I could go log it in. I forgot myself once
and told Olympia, "The program says you need another four ounces of
water before dinner."

She looked at me like I'd spoken in Vietnamese. "What?"

"Nothing," I mumbled.

The idea was to make the process invisible. Mostly, Olympia just
showed up. And ate. And sulked. But she sulked a little less every day.

The nutritionist we consulted for her expertise and experience with eating disorders reluctantly divulged that 3,500 calories a day would be necessary to refeed Olympia at home. She was "skeptical" that Olympia could do this without hospitalization and was not familiar with or encouraging about the Maudsley concept. Actually, she was dismissive. When we told her that we were no longer waiting for Olympia to "choose" to eat, the nutritionist's tone changed. Our daughter might become defiant, she might "think of running away," she warned. I remembered the children's book *The Runaway Bunny*: " 'If you run away,' says the mother, 'I will run after you. For you are my little bunny.' "

As though running away were a valid and understandable response to your parents expecting you to eat. As though children whose parents watch them starve were more attractive. As though anorexia were a matter of taste and judgment, like piercing your navel or taking up cigarettes.

It was a draw with the nutritionist; we just made no more appointments and she never called to ask why. Since she wasn't interested in giving me specifics, I went to the sources. Medical and professional journals laid nuggets of information in my path: case studies, tables, clinical examples. The nitty-gritty details of treatment in clinics and hospitals are not readily available, but I gleaned enough to give us clues—and to scare myself silly.

I read with horror about refeeding syndrome, in which the anorexic patient experiences heart and metabolic problems from being refed too quickly. Luckily we were well into refeeding by the time I read that, but I wondered why none of the people we had consulted mentioned it. I can only guess that they never believed Olympia would begin to eat while she lived at home.

I learned that the body of an anorexic, when receiving the full nutrition it needs, initially overmetabolizes in a frenzied joy to see real food. This both speeds up the metabolism and requires more food, but it also freaks out the poor anorexic who is anxious enough by being tortured with double-fudge smoothies at every turn.

Not only does your food-phobic anorexic have to eat, but she has to eat amounts most sumo wrestlers might blush over. Again, no advice was out there on how to deal with this quandary, but having read about it, at least we were not blindsided.

It is even possible to reach a state in which there is no way to consume enough calories to add weight. I was thankful for finding that gem, as it explained why Olympia's weight gain slowed after a steady gain. It kept us from blaming her and from suspecting that she was secretly exercising or purging. There was no manual for parents to do this, no handbook. Parents are not trusted to refeed anorexics. They are only trusted to starve them.

NONE OF THE INFORMATION I found was meant for us. I spent hundreds of dollars buying reprints of articles and months reading a backlog of journals with names like *Molecular Psychiatry* and *European Journal of Endocrinology*. This isn't something most parents are inclined or encouraged to do. I did it because I've always been told to back off and relax when it comes to my kids, but I've never regretted it when I didn't. I did it because I could, but it scared me for those who could not. It still does.

Meanwhile, Samuel and I learned the exact calories of a hundred foods. We ate huge, hearty meals, and Elijah touched down as much as he could—especially with dessert as an incentive. We took everything our diet-conscious society has taught us and turned it upside down.

We weighed Olympia once a week. More often seemed silly and too stressful for all of us, although the scientist in me would have liked the data. We picked Saturday morning to let any emotional fallout from the increased weight play out at home instead of at school. We tried not to inconvenience her.

Olympia approached the scale like a gallows. Regardless of the numbers indicated, we all kept straight faces. She would sometimes go off and cry. We would stay behind and resist a high five. The scale was our paycheck. And her guillotine.

Her weight went down only once from the time we began refeeding. It was only a pound, and we let it slide. I swallowed my terror. Samuel left his suspicions unspoken. Olympia said nothing. The next week she was up two and a half pounds. It gently rose from then on—and so did her mood.

18

PAY NO ATTENTION TO THE MAN
BEHIND THE CURTAIN!

You don't believe me, do you? I know what you're thinking: "You can't just make an anorexic eat."

When we rejected—and were rejected by—the traditional and available route of anorexia treatment, we had to fall back on a very authoritarian lifestyle: we say it, you do it. Luckily, we were qualified. Not one of our parents ever tried to be our best friend: they were loving parents, they knew best—or at least had the car keys. This is a very unpopular style of parenting now among our peers, and it wasn't our habit, but we sure could do it when needed.

Samuel was Ward and I was June and that was that.

Critics of our family's approach call it "force feeding," but I call it "supported nutrition." And remembering the fear that Olympia showed at the beginning of her illness, we operated under the belief that she needed our complete confidence and our absolute authority, to be able to trust us. We promised to feed her, but not to overfeed her. Like a girl in the middle of a windstorm she mostly followed the sound of our voices, trusting, even in her terror, that we would not let her down.

The first meals were comical. She pushed things around on the plate, cut things into mash. We didn't budge. We allowed her to leave 10 percent on the plate to give a sense of self-control (I read they do this on eating disorder wards), but no one got up until the meal was done. Our meals slowed into marathons. It was hard to know when one meal ended and another began.

After these tortured meals, for the first few weeks, Samuel would take Elijah away, and Olympia would sob, rage, and beg. There was nothing to do but sit by, and afterward I would be allowed to embrace her. Sometimes. Her physical and emotional pain were terrifying. I tried not to take the things she said or the way she acted personally. I was impassive. I was steady. And then, alone, I took my turn and cried while Samuel stood in as the bionic parent.

Meals became more belligerent as she regained her strength. She was nasty, short-tempered, silent. We ignored it. Grief was to be borne on the couch. She was not allowed to be alone, not allowed in the bathroom. No closed doors. No exercise. There was, however, anger between meals. We stood it.

We did not need her to like it. Or to like us. She could hate us with all her breath as long as it was between bites.

At first the agonies took hours to subside. They took so long that it was a while before I realized there was less and less pain each day. Increments so tiny only I could see them, and I wondered if I was losing touch with reality, too. These were the dividends, meager as they were, that kept me from despair. With the knowledge that the physical damage was receding with every meal eaten and with the lightening of the emotional agony, I held onto the hope that we were doing the right thing.

There is a shift, subtle but substantive, when you stop seeing a behavior as a choice and start seeing it as a medical, physical, somatically driven problem. The blame ends. The guilt stops cold. You are back on the same side as your loved one—even if she doesn't know it yet.

COMPARE IT TO BEING A DIABETIC, but at a time when the experts and the people you love insist you are just making yourself weak. They are angry with your choice to feel ill. They feel guilty for teaching you to have low blood sugar. And while your pancreas expires, you are left to discover the "underlying" issue behind your immature craving for glucose. Making an anorexic choose whether or not to eat is little different.

We are often asked, "How did you get her to eat?" We answer that we left her no choice. We gave her emotional support before, during, and after meals, but we negotiated nothing. The food was served, no choices were offered, and the food had to be consumed. When she balked, we were silent. If she left the table, we told her we would stay there until she came back. She tried it; she came back. She could not get on the bus, go alone to her room, or resume normal life until the meal was taken and settled. No fighting. No compromising. We laid it out, and she knew we would stand by it.

We took the decision making out of her hands and allowed her to heal. I cannot pretend to understand what was going on in her head— although I listened—but it didn't matter. Eating was not optional.

Parents tell me they are afraid to lose the little bit their anorexic is eating. They fear the child will stop going to school, will run away, will hate them. They fear the uncharacteristic behavior of their child when confronted over food. It is not easy to change the basic agreements of modern parent and child, but Samuel and I could see that this disease was life-threatening and that our daughter was no longer rational. We would have stopped school, friends, phone, TV, having a room of her own, even her ever being alone.

And of course, we reminded her, there was the hospital.

As it was, the regimen changed our lives. Being aware of mealtimes, of amounts, and of the atmosphere around them—every day of every week of every month—is surprisingly exhausting. It was almost a year to the day she stopped eating before we were forced into a mealtime we could neither serve nor plan for. By that time she could—and did—do it on her own.

Other parents who hear our story think Olympia was just less ill than their child. I believe they are wrong. We started early—within weeks of the severe restriction. We had a strong relationship with our daughter to start with, and that helped. Samuel and I were also a united front, once the decision was made, and had no one to undermine us once the therapist and nutritionist were out of the picture. We had the luxury of time and money: I was able to stop working and be home, and we were able to buy a variety of interesting food, as well as to eat out at will. We had the specter of other people's stories of repeated hospitalizations, illness, and death to motivate us. And most importantly, we had the will and ability to bring life down to its most basic level—food, clothing, shelter—to save our daughter's life.

When Olympia first became ill, she expressed feelings that were frightening to hear. She did not conceal them or lie. She was frightened, very frightened, and begged us for help if not for food.

"I feel sick."

"It's all growing. Everywhere. I feel it growing." She clutched compulsively at the loose skin of her stomach and the inside of her arms. Pinching. Bruising.

"I'm scared, Mom. I'm scared. What's wrong with me? I used to be OK, right? Don't be angry."

We were fortunate. The next two months were awful, but at least the lines of communication stayed open. I hated to hear it all, it was frightening, and I did not always react in the right way, but she still trusted us at some basic level. Perhaps it was because we didn't blame her and we didn't give up. I am thankful.

BREAKFASTS IMPROVED FIRST. She started to awaken grimly ready to eat and didn't complain until the end, and we learned to hear her out with passive faces. Then she and I started to enjoy getting up early and eating together before school. I hated myself for having let her get her own breakfast in previous years. At the time I thought I was giving her independence. Now I realize I missed out on a wonderful time for just the two of us.

Lunch at school was a problem. We agreed to let her eat there if she was honest about what she ate and her weight didn't go down. Our agreement was that if her weight dropped, we would pick her up at school and eat with her in the car. This mortified her. But she also knew we weren't bluffing. Amazingly, sometimes she would report having eaten very little at lunchtime, something she easily could have fudged. I added a cookie to the snack on those days.

The increments of improvement in mood and attitude about food were small. But there came a day when she came home and said, "What's for snack? I'm hungry." And a day in a friend's car that she accepted a candy, and then ate it.

One day after she reached a healthy weight, after four months, she asked me, almost sheepishly, "Is this how I looked . . . before?"

"Yes."

"Oh."

The look in her eyes, when she understood at that moment that the feeling of being strangely too big had been a delusion, was extremely hard to watch. I wish I could have taken it away from her, erased it. The realization of how sick she had been—and the unreality of it—was crushing. I had felt scared, angry, tired, and frustrated, but not until that moment did the profound sadness hit me fully.

Olympia was as afraid of overeating as of not eating. All she could think of was food, but if she chose a bite it was as if she were choosing a mountain of food. Eating only made her hungrier and desperate for more, and she felt ashamed. Released from the decisions, she was able to eat, and as her mind released the anxiety, to relearn listening to hunger, and to satiation.

THE FIRST STAGE OF REFEEDING was excruciating for all of us. She was being tortured, it was obvious. She hated us. She was disgusted with us.

It was only the clear, unblindered conviction that she was not rational and we were that made it possible to look into her contemptuous eyes and not back down. The disease was not her.

"She is in there," I told myself. "We will get her back."

But I had no way of "knowing" that. I had only a handful of journal articles, some scattered comments quoted in the press, some inferences from professional discussions, and my gut instincts. My husband was depending on me to know what I was doing with all these ideas and theories. He trusted me. Olympia was trusting me. But we were working without a net.

Somewhere along the line we did find a specialist who believed in the Maudsley approach. Dr. Tomas Silber, at Children's National Medical Center in Washington, D.C., became our long-distance sanity check. As an adolescent medicine specialist with an interest in eating disorders, Dr. Silber knew the literature and knew the disease. Olympia liked him. Samuel liked him. I loved him instantly for the way he looked Olympia in the eye and did not laugh at my sheaf of research notes. He did not think our feeding Olympia was wrong. He talked with all of us together, encouraged us, cheered us on as a family. I'd like to clone him and give him out as a gift to every parent: "To be opened in case of emergency."

Dr. Silber doesn't think the Maudsley approach is for everyone, only for parents "who are not afraid of their children."

The process of recovery is very slow. The popular wisdom is that anorexia takes five to seven years to subside. I question the statistic, but accept this reality: it wasn't a week or a month or even six months before we saw something even resembling normality. And we had no idea what to expect. Every day was another three ("plus snack") lines in the sand. Every day was a step away from the worst, hoping that the future would be better.

JUST BECAUSE WE COULD NO LONGER ARGUE with our daughter about food didn't take the sport entirely out of the house. Samuel and I became crazy people in the kitchen. We could be found before dinner whispering and waving utensils as we debated the relative merits of cheesecake and ice cream, how much comprises an ounce, and whether ten small items were better than two big items. We did all this insanity in secret, in hushed tones. We knew food preparation made Olympia anxious, so we just made it happen without her watching or participating. Until it became true, with habit and time, we maintained the fiction that for our family, food was a natural and pleasant affair. We set a table heretofore unimaginable, and then called our offspring to the table as if it had been delivered by a maid.

It was of utmost importance that neither Samuel nor I be caught not eating. We became monstrous and conspicuous gluttons. Madly, gladly, ravenously eating. We were calling her into the water: "Look, honey, it's safe! The water is fine!" Splash, splash, chew, chew. The lengths to which we went to model hearty eating were transparently comic. Constantly stuffed, I found myself reviewing with no little interest the ways anorexics hide food, and avoid eating.

"But, that would be bad," I thought wistfully.

So I shoveled.

Samuel ignored my stressed-out twitch when he repeatedly leapt up for a different condiment, ruining my tableau. I ignored the way Elijah practiced newfound belching skills. Good-natured Samuel took no offense when I castigated him in high-pitched whispers in the hallway for portions I thought were too small or too big. Elijah, ebullience incarnate, ignored us all and went about his life. And Olympia grimly—and eventually with amusement—pretended we hadn't lost our minds.

I don't believe our family's eating habits gave our daughter anorexia. Different habits would probably just have delayed it until a stressful future date in which she ate too little or exercised too much. But maybe our formerly lackadaisical attitude about food actually helped: we were flexible enough to change and refeed her.

New rituals joined us at the table. We said the Hebrew blessing more often and inserted absurd things we were thankful for. Elijah began asking for fables with him as the star, for which Olympia would provide sound effects. Everyone was asked about their day. Ward and June were very happy. Actually, eventually, we were all very happy at the table, eating with our anorexic.

19

FEMINIST TURNS INTO
DONNA REED—DETAILS AT 11

THE FIRST PROBLEM with our new program was learning to cook.

I don't mean that Samuel and I didn't know how to cook dishes of food. We had just never been good at composing whole meals—meals comprised of several food groups and served at the table with beverages, utensils, salt and pepper, and dessert. We certainly hadn't done that more than once a week, not to mention three meals a day plus snack. As strange, and possibly pathological, as it sounds, that seemed like a nearly impossible goal. For our eclectic, spontaneous, inefficient little family it seemed like we were adopting a ritual of labyrinthine complexity.

Before anorexia, we called our version of mealtime "free for all" dinners. What that really meant was that neither Samuel nor I had given a thought to feeding us all, until we were hungry. We expected the kids to tell us when they were hungry. If a grand inspiration seized us we might whip up something for everyone, but even then it might be four bowls of cereal or plates of cheese and pickles and too many peanut butter sandwiches.

Early in our marriage I tried to do the model family thing and enforce meals, but it never took. Samuel left the house before we woke up in the morning. Olympia and I snacked during the day as the mood struck. None of us were ever hungry for dinner at the same time. None of us ever ate the same foods or had the same hunger rhythms. We were never together for mealtimes, or always on our way somewhere, or having too many people to fit at the table, or watching a movie. Our only family dinners were at restaurants.

Elijah's arrival and temperament obliterated the few sit-down opportunities we would have had. As a baby he was unable to sleep on schedule and unwilling to eat on one either. He couldn't sit still while we ate, and later he didn't sit still to eat anywhere. Restaurant meals, which we only began to afford with regularity around the time Elijah was born, became moot with a baby who could not occupy the same space for more than 120 seconds.

I know this sounds unhealthy, but it worked for us at the time.

Our kids were so good at being happy, healthy eaters that Olympia's illness blindsided us badly. I had never forced her to finish her plate, never fixed her plates piled with food, never served desserts as some incentive to eat healthy meals beforehand. I had little experience with making large meals and serving them. I had never anticipated anyone's hunger or level of satiation. I knew how to follow, but not to lead. But suddenly my child was unable to tell me what she wanted to eat, or when, or how much.

Clumsily, frantically, a routine set in. Strict times were established for breakfast, lunch, and dinner. Samuel would preside over the meal with attempts at humor; I played the straight man with little effort, as I could see little to laugh about. Olympia would stonily comply with repeated demands that she resume eating through her tears. Elijah, unused to and temperamentally unsuited to mealtime calm, would spin in his seat, under the table, and around the room, which elicited time-outs and hissed warnings that put the lie to the happy family dinner we were pretending to have.

I needed a Donna Reed lesson in a hurry. My mother, the college professor and professional dinner guest, had long ago happily abdicated domesticity. I was too busy being a brat to my stepmother when she was a stay-at-home mother to have taken any notes. My two fathers each had their own specialty: "broiled chicken thighs marinated in soy sauce" and "macaroni and cheese with peas and tuna," respectively. This was a job for Mother-In-Law.

Lucky for me, my mother-in-law has retained her graciousness, which includes "forgetting" any former discord with her headstrong daughter-in-law, and the good housekeeping habits of her young married life, which includes knowing how to cook well, efficiently, and abundantly. She delivered recipes, weekly pep talks, cheering e-mails, and hundreds of packages of frozen pesto pasta, macaronis, loaves of braided bread, lemon and poppyseed cakes, hamantaschen, kugel. Dina's house was the only place, for a long while, that we could bring Olympia for a meal. Her home was a place where filling the plates in the kitchen was not strange, where dessert was not an afterthought, where the grandparental authority commanded that food be eaten with joy and some class.

Olympia's anorexia terrified us all, but Dina was the one, in the end, with the skills that we lacked. The first time Olympia slept away from home since her illness was at Dina's. I had a whispered call after dessert, saying "She had an extra green bean." We both cried. A spontaneous additional helping, even of a bean, was like sighting the first bloom of spring. Olympia was coming back.

Anorexia brought me back to my cultural roots. I married into Jewish food-pushing, but I had some right to believe it was my genetic heritage as well. Although my parents were lackluster at food-seduction, I believe my African-American and Irish antecedents offer me membership in the nooge militia. And I took anyone else's roots I could adopt to get the job done—my in-law's, my college roommate's, the Italians, the French—heck, whatever worked. I was willing to sign on to whatever cultural or ethnic or religious ancestry would achieve our goals. I had the feeling that no single tradition had the capacity to bring my daughter back to health on its own.

Olympia had to eat a bucket of calories a day, and we had to get it in her. She'd look at these ridiculous mounds of food and look at us as if to say "You people do realize that I am an *anorexic*, right? I mean, did you mistake me for a linebacker? A bulimic? Get with the program, people! Anorexics don't eat. Read the manual."

You would be surprised how much butter can be put into a day. Butter became our main food group. Butter can be hidden in things as varied as oatmeal and hamburger. I can make scrambled eggs that have as much butter as egg yolk. I put butter in her warm milk.

Ensure is designed for old people and cancer patients. No one thinks of it as a supplement for high school sophomores in bell bottoms. But over ice it's not so bad. It comes in flavors. I think her friends thought it was a diet drink. It's not funny. Stop laughing.

I learned a lot by trolling sites on the Internet for cancer patients. There are special high-calorie diets out there for people sick from chemotherapy. They didn't have enough calories, but I learned some tips. Whipped cream has forty calories per dollop; a corn muffin can deliver more than five hundred. Nowhere in our pantry could you find the words "low-fat" or "sugar free." We retrofitted our lives and our diet to the 1950s and we were swinging.

When you add calories instead of trimming them you're cheating in this wonderful, clandestine way. You take a secret delight in adding a quarter portion. You think of using milk—no, cream!—instead of water in recipes. You consider dried fruits to be vitamin tablets. You think of foods as rich in nutrients instead of fattening. Food becomes wholesome and healthy and whole again.

I'll bet you haven't heard that for a while.

20

LIKE A LAB SHEDS WATER

"Just eat it!" he said as he left the table.

Samuel is the son of a Jewish mother. He's used to seeing people eat. Sometimes he just got tired and angry.

We could see him struggling during the dinner itself. He couldn't help staring at Olympia's plate, asking about how the food tasted, worrying about whether she liked it. It was driving him crazy. He was the king of our table—the chef, the chief entertainer, the provider—and she was eating so slowly.

He knew intellectually what the plan was. To be calm, to fill Olympia's plate and set it out. No asking if she wanted seconds. No forcing her to make choices. No stealing a bite of her carefully calibrated portions. No lecturing. I would kick him under the table when he slipped into annoyance at her rituals: the careful cutting away of fat from meat, the portion of each item left on the plate, and the tiny bites.

"It is melting!" he finally exploded as she perched amounts of ice cream the size of pinto beans on the tip of her spoon. It was liquid before it reached her lips. "I can't watch."

I stayed and watched what annoyed and frightened him. I felt torn between her efforts to get well and his need to get away.

He would forget our careful rules and all their very sound rationales. He would forget Maudsley and refeeding and often seemed to forget anorexia itself. He was just too normal. I was so pathetically adaptable that I could see and do everything under this safe, supportive, but ultimately quite strange new filter. Samuel was normal every single day, and it was a strain to keep reminding himself to be strange.

He is an active man, a sportsman, a career-driven and hardworking father. He only felt helpless when there was nothing for him to do. He calls it "a guy response." He needed action. "I have to see, smell, touch, and taste things." And he did. He cooked as if it were now his profession. He shopped for groceries like Santa Claus. He stocked the pantry, refilled the grill's propane tanks, drove out of his way for supplies and tempting condiments. He took Elijah out in the woods, out on the water, in the backyard, to wash the car, out of the way. He did things.

He had little patience for talking. I did the talking. I did the passive listening. I comforted and sustained and affirmed and kept my temper. Mostly. Well, as much as I could.

When it came to conversation he stayed silent and then blasted. He laid out the battle plan. "All life stops unless you are cured," he said. "You are going to die if you don't eat."

Those were words I could not say.

Samuel and Olympia like to drive places together. They like going to movies, running a specific errand, dropping by Grandma's. In the car together, where the two of them have always had their best conversations, they discussed things I did not preapprove. He said things that were not vetted through my strict program controls. He went off message and off topic and outside our little box. It was then that she asked him things she must not have thought I could handle. From me she got the soft landing. From him she got the hard line.

I was all about the program, the plan, the right things to do, to say, to work toward. My universe was bounded by so many things that "we cannot do" and "we must not say."

Samuel will always be the one with the long view. People have kids; kids grow up and go away; kids have kids and grandparents get to point and laugh.

We were a good team.

"Well, we went into the game strong," he used an active analogy, of course, to explain why our marriage kept us going and kept itself going. The emotional travail between Olympia and me was like a game he couldn't follow. He sometimes finds people too messy, too complicated; he prefers the company of dogs. Especially the breeds that eat heartily and live for another meal.

He didn't bother blaming himself. He didn't blame me.

He didn't care what people thought of him or of what we did.

He says we did what we did because you just do. "Not that complicated. Besides, she was shedding weight like a Labrador sheds water."

I love this man.

21

BLINKING MADLY

As a child, I learned that if I found myself in a nightmare I could still escape from whatever demon or gargoyle pursued me. The trick was to turn around and face the demon directly, stomp my feet a ritual number of times, then blink exactly three times. Eventually I learned that the stomping was not necessary. In time it turned out that a single blink sufficed, since blinking a closed eye in a dream opens it in reality.

Eating disorder treatments from intensive outpatient to long-term residential—and of course the Maudsley approach—share a common factor: the patient eats and doesn't purge. They also throw in an à la carte menu of additional therapies, group sessions, nutritional counseling, family week, and art therapy.

What about just blinking?

Plenty of methods have been used on anorexics. The original anorexia theorist, Sir William Gull, might fit in quite easily with the Maudsleyans of today. He prescribed full nutrition over as long a period as needed, use of a trained nurse at home, optimism, warm bed rest, and lots of protein and calcium. He stated, "The inclination of the patient must in no way be consulted."

The Mitchell Method featured massage and milk.

Freudians and their descendants employed psychoanalysis.

More recently, those who have eating disorders have been isolated in hospitals, clinics, and residential treatment centers where they are refed and given therapy. Through behavioral therapy they are taught new ways to act. In interpersonal therapy they learn how to better relate to others. Traditional psychotherapy addresses "underlying" issues. Nutritional counseling teaches healthy eating. Cognitive approaches attempt to retrain the brain to abandon negative thought patterns.

There are even newer therapies: dialectical behavior therapy, narrative therapy, and several other flavors of the month.

The rates of recovery have always been dismal. The theories change. New ones arise perennially. Unfortunately, no one seems to be in charge of clearing away the ones that no longer make any sense.

ONE OF THE THEORIES on the origins of anorexia is that it may be set in motion by malnutrition. Some percentage of the population may have a problem with dieting because of overmetabolism of a neurotransmitter, like norepinephrine, or of a nutrient, like zinc. This is a harmless condition while the brain is fully fed, but it could spiral out of control under low levels of dietary nutrients. Once initiated, the impulses become obsessive and self-perpetuating. The sufferer, if allowed to starve, is unable to regain equilibrium because she cannot eat. Another explanation for why an anorexic cannot easily resume eating is that her body has forgotten how: the complex physiological feedback system misfires, stutters, and forgets where it was.

The most satisfying theory I know was conceived by a psychologist in Montana, who for some reason is able to cut through all the past and present of this disease and see this: evolution had a purpose for anorexics. Shan Guisinger's "Adapted to Flee Famine Hypothesis" will be unattractive to strict creationists, Freudians, and those who have crawled out of their disease the hard, long, and repeatedly hospitalized way. But through the lens of evolution I can see anorexics themselves finding comfort—and perhaps a path out—in the understanding that certain people may be designed, in the presence of starvation (even voluntary), to turn off their own survival instincts to protect their family and extended gene pool.

Anorexics who anxiously prepare elaborate feasts for their families while themselves abstaining will recognize the Neanderthal woman who sets out into the savannah to seek food and relate to her pride as she drags back a mastodon leg for her brood. Our modern anorexic may recognize the animal models Guisinger cites: migrating animals whose appetites are suppressed until their families are safe, rats who become hyperactive after falling to 70 percent of their normal body weight.

The twenty-first-century anorexic, however, will not experience the homecoming and cheers her Pleistocene sisters would have received as she returned, triumphant, with a skirtful of supplies. He will not be welcomed and nurtured back to health by his thankful relatives. The modern anorexic is first admired, then bitterly envied, and finally left to his or her own strange atavistic devices.

There are many theories about possible biological triggers: extreme stress flooding the system with cortisol, an autoimmune malfunction, pheromonal dysregulation, lipid dysregulation, rapid changes in hormonal activity during puberty, blood sugar malfunction, brain-derived neurotrophic factor (BDNF) deficiency, or just simple dietary deficiency. But the majority of anorexics recover their senses with the reacquisition of their former physical health through eating. This is especially true if the refeeding starts quickly. And it doesn't need to be voluntary.

THERE IS NOTHING WRONG with support groups, self-help books, affirmations, and improving one's life. Good therapy improves us, strengthens us. Dealing with past trauma, losses, and damage is inherently good. Unless that is all you get. Unless these approaches replace treatment of the body living with these diseases, leaving that body to the ravages of starvation, malnutrition, or purging. Not for one day. Not for one meal. And none of those pleasant interventions are good if they teach you to blame something for your illness that is not true. Or if they cause you to believe you would not have had an eating disorder if you had only done these fine things before.

In other words, nothing had to be broken in the first place for you to get anorexia. You need not have lived in a dysfunctional home, been sexually abused, or been bullied at school. You may have had just as functional, loving, and nurturing a childhood as your parents thought they gave you. Knowing that, parents can be freed to continue loving their children, nurturing them and supporting them through a grave and vicious illness not of their own choosing. Parents do not have to wait, in agony, for the child or her other keepers to let them.

Why should you eat with your anorexic? Because you are the best qualified and the most committed. Because it works. And because, truly, it tastes terrific.

22

"CREEPY, CRUEL, AND HIGHLY DISTURBING"

I'm ODDLY PROUD of having elicited comments like "creepy, cruel, and highly disturbing." Those are fighting words. They crystallize the sentiment that neatly splits the different camps of thought on treating eating disorders. Those words were said of Samuel and me and of family-based refeeding, but I have grown increasingly willing to say the same of the other camp.

Here are the schools of thought about treating eating disorders, and anorexia in particular:

School A: When the sufferer is ready to seek help, uncover and heal the underlying emotional and developmental issues that caused the behaviors; only then will the behaviors be truly abandoned and the person healed.

School B: Stop the behaviors as soon as possible, by whatever means are best for that individual, and after physical stabilization begin therapy to understand the underlying motivations.

School Me: Protect the sufferer from the behaviors as soon as possible, by whatever means are best for that individual; support them through the anguish the disease is causing; treat the physical imbalances that have caused or worsened the illness; and reinforce the individual's emotional support system both internally and externally.

School A is widely practiced in therapy and treatment in the United States. School B is a rudely rendered distillation of the Maudsley approach, which is used in the United Kingdom. And you already know me.

What we did with Olympia is referred to by some in School A as "forceful breaking of the sufferer's will" and "aggressive refeeding." When my critics are feeling charitable, they refer to my daughter as "more compliant" or "less ill."

School A believes that anorexia is a way for a distressed person to gain some control in her life. They say that anorexics "must choose to get well" and that "sometimes they have to hit bottom to seek help."

I believe this is extraordinarily cruel. Here's my bottom line: you either believe anorexia is "refusing" to eat or you believe anorexia is the "inability" to eat. That is the dividing line, and you have to choose a side.

If you believe anorexics choose not to eat, you talk and rage and sometimes give up. If you believe they can't eat, you lovingly make the decision for them until they can.

Although nearly everyone now throws in the giveaway line "genetic component" when talking about anorexia, they don't seem to believe it. Who would want to? I'd love to believe my daughter chose this behavior and could choose her way out of it. I'd love to think that this was a stage she went through and will now know her way around. I would even accept full responsibility for causing and exacerbating her illness if I thought it would cure her. Believe me, I did not enjoy the day I first said to her that what she was experiencing was a mental illness. Yet as scary as mental illnesses sound, diseases like depression and bipolar disorder are no longer the frightening and intractable things they once were. Anorexia may, with sound research, someday be a brief and less harmful disease.

Of course, believing this disease is really just a lapse in thinking, a cognitive wrong turn in the road, or a somehow understandable response to crippling events—this appeals to our American conception of ourselves as independent and self-actualizing beings. The idea that we can—and must—talk ourselves out of it is something we apply to so much of our lives and actions and ideals. We want to be masters of our destiny. We want our loved ones to embrace life.

But there are limits. I cannot breathe underwater. I can't make myself grow to seven feet tall by force of will. I cannot compute polynomial equations in my head.

And I cannot give myself anorexia nervosa. Neither did my daughter. Nor did she choose to get better. Only after months of supported refeeding did she recover emotionally. Released from the fear her body put her through during food choices, she was able to deconstruct the delusional and irrational thoughts that still seized her. Very slowly, she regained her sanity. It took four months to repair the immediate effects of two months of starvation, six months to see a real improvement in her mood. It was a year before she could reliably talk rationally about her body, food, and her future.

And no, she is not the same person as before.

I didn't say it was easy.

School A accuses me of discounting free will, of making my daughter sicker with my control over her actions. They call me mechanistic and cruel.

It's time to turn this idea on its head. It's time to call it cruel to insist that a person who is operating under a hallucinatory delusion needs to "choose" not to see it. It's time to call it creepy to label when a loved one is actively hurting himself as individuation.

This will probably shock those who have never encountered an eating disorder, but there are families who hear, find evidence of, and even sometimes see their child vomiting after meals, and who think they should not do anything—or even mention it. There are parents who hide groceries to keep them from their bingeing children and spend thousands of extra dollars on food purged into clogged drains, but who do not believe they have a role in stopping the behavior. Parents all over the United States sit at dinner with their children, well aware those children have eaten nothing all day, and watch them eat a single bite of salad and say they are full. The parents then get up from the table to go cry in their room. They have been told not to get involved, not to make a fuss, not to say anything. They are to leave it to the professionals.

I read it, I heard it, and to my great shame, I believed it. For the first few weeks of my daughter's madness, I went along—it was a strange, theatric, out-of-body experience. I was frantic at the sight of her strange eyes and her weakening body, but I thought I was supposed to act indifferent and nonjudgmental, and so I did.

I was not indifferent, though, and I should not have acted as if I were. What was happening to Olympia was bizarre, outlandish, and pathological. By acting normal I was betraying her trust that I, at least, was sane, and that we would keep her safe. And every single meal she did not eat made her sicker.

What must it be like to live suddenly in a world that presents a mind-blowing phobia several times a day? It would be like being forced to drape myself with rattlesnakes every six hours for the rest of my life. I'd go to awful lengths to avoid that. I'd hide, run, lie, and say awful things to the people forcing me to do that. Even if the snakes were keeping me alive.

Eating is not a poisonous serpent, though. It really is necessary to live. Some of us even like it. The less you eat, the sicker you get. Allowing someone to opt out of eating or to eat only certain foods that don't add up to a day's energy and nutrient supply—why is this a choice?

And what should we think, really, of a world that accepts that choice? Ask yourself what anorexics must think of the world they used to trust, in that small, still-rational part of their brain.

If my daughter were drowning I would pull her out. If she were taking a bottle of barbiturates, I would have her stomach pumped. You might even accuse me of "force living" my child.

I suspect that the control issues displayed in an eating disorder are another symptom and not its cause. The perfectionist personality, the low self-esteem, and the fear of fat are all symptoms of a common factor, such as glands or hormones or a neurotransmitter gone awry—or a pathologic orgy of them all.

People shouldn't need to choose to get well to get help. They deserve to be fully fed, for a long time, and to be supported emotionally and practically while they heal. It is cruel to wait until they choose. Let's take the knife out of their hand, pull them off the ledge. Is that so controlling?

"I can't make her eat! I don't want to be the Food Police!" you say.

Ah, the practical issues. Not everyone can drop everything to care for a sick child. I mean, if your son got cancer and you had no one to bring him to chemo, you would just let him die, right? If your daughter is holding a knife and you've got to catch the train to work, well, that's her choice, right? A sucking wound in the chest, well, that will teach you to play with guns.

"How extreme! How can you compare eating disorders to cancer? This is different. What kind of person do you think I am?" I can hear you saying.

I think you are someone who thinks of eating disorders as a choice, not as an involuntary and life-threatening illness like cancer, but attacking the brain instead of the liver or the blood. You would get leave from work or get twenty-four-hour care for your mother who suffers from Alzheimer's, but you think this is different because anorexics can stop it if they choose to. But I think people who are actively throwing up their meals or eating limp grasses for lunch are too ill to be left to make their own decisions. I think you have been given wrong information, and I'm sorry.

I think we live in a society that thinks of growing up as a one-way path and sees parents as a launching missile designed to fall off in prescribed stages. I think we worship choice and free will to the point where we will let mentally ill people suffer in some misguided effort to maintain their dignity. I think we confuse control over food in eating disorders with the normal struggle we all have over food. And I think it is wrong.

"It isn't about food," you say.

True. It is about mental illness. It is about suffering. And it is cruel, creepy, and disturbing to leave people to suffer with it unsupported because they tell us they don't want our help.

By leaving our daughter no choice but to eat, strange and artificial as it was, we acted sanely. By treating full nutrition and emotional support as medicine, we reaffirmed our daughter's dignity as a human being and her right to live and trust the people around her. Until she was ready—and eventually she was—to embrace her own recovery, we held the world up for her. I'd do it again.

Honey, I'd do it again.

23

NATURE VERSUS NURTURE

THE EATING DISORDER INDUSTRY—and the mental health field as a whole—is shifting to a view of eating disorders as biologically based mental illnesses. But this shift has not reached everyone yet. I believe the professionals don't really mean to deceive or mismanage their patients. It's probably just that they've seen these kinds of things—scientific explanations and theories about brain chemistry—before. The mental health professions have been through this "psych versus soma" battle before.

Once upon a time, the "mad" were cared for by their families at home unless or until they were institutionalized by the authorities. In the bad mad days, unspeakable medical treatments were administered to these unfortunates—experiments that predated and outlived Hitler. Sometimes with good intentions but often with shocking disregard for the humans concerned, patients were doused, heated, chilled, fried, and chopped in the name of mental hygiene. This left a very bad taste in the profession's collective mouth and caused a shift to a humanistic and fuzzier era of mental health care. This newer, kinder era of psychiatry also meshed well with a realization that the population of mental health institutions had been disproportionately drawn from people with less capital and more melanin. It is no wonder that new people entering the field were loath to be associated with genetic determinism and biological tomfoolery.

My father obviously didn't hear about that shift.

In the days before animal researchers needed bodyguards, my mild-mannered and crew-cutted father was bringing me pet rats from the psych lab with their cute little electrode wires still dangling. I'm sure the PETA squad would like to test perfumes on his eyeballs, but my dad learned a lot while studying the brain. As a result, my childhood was spent receiving a graduate seminar on "nature vs. nurture" in human behavior. In our debates I usually played the "nurture" side while he argued "nature."

As usual, you never know how smart your parents are until you are one yourself.

I love my father very much. (Actually, I have two, this one just came first.) I love him so much I would protect him from any pain I could avoid inflicting. He is the last person I would want to worry about his dear oldest granddaughter. He was one of the first people I called.

"I can't believe they are still selling that psychological stuff. They were arguing that in 1969," he said of the way Olympia's therapist and doctors seemed to see her anorexia as a choice she was making. He was shocked to learn that anorexia was still being treated as if it were not a biologically triggered mental illness. He explained that there was a longtime disconnect between the clinicians who see patients and the researchers with the rodents. He sighed, "I loved to hang out with the 'people people,' but my money was on the brain people all the way."

It was a good phone call. I felt less alone in my suspicions that this disease was not the voice of my daughter's subconscious yearning to be childlike as well as free of her parents. My childhood indoctrination in biological psychiatry worked. And now I had one more good brain on my side.

It was clear early on that the answers—and even the questions—were not going to be delivered to us on the tongue of a therapist or found in some ultimate holy text.

From my crying command tower, I became a full-time researcher. I did my research as though someone's life depended on it. At first it seemed presumptuous to be writing and calling professors and researchers around the world to track down leads and papers and conference proceedings. After all, I'm just a mother. I found the phrase "my daughter is dying" is an excellent way to embolden a mom. I learned where to look, how to read, and what the patterns are. My fan mail/data requests were, strangely, almost always answered. Which is not to say that I was welcomed into the fraternity, but parents on a rampage are disarming on two levels: one, they are not as common as you might think; and two, what more earnest goal could there be than saving one's child?

My husband, who managed to keep his mind on his work—and off the "problem"—enough to keep his job, was entirely supportive. He started talking about groundbreaking work and *Lorenzo's Oil*, a movie about a mother who defied her child's doctors and saved her son's life. I managed to wait until his third reference to that brave and fierce mother to mention that the eponymous Lorenzo is still completely disabled and his mother is dead.

Although our daughter was now eating and was regaining her sanity along with her health, we were in uncharted territory without a guide. Olympia was physically stable within a month of refeeding, back to her original weight in four months, and cleared for knee surgery shortly thereafter. But what about the future? What about cause and preventing relapse? We were feeding her now, but would she ever be able to feed herself? And when?

Even still, I was happy for one more meal, one pound a week, and the glimmer of evidence that Olympia's delusions were receding.

"When's dinner?" she would ask. This is anorexic treason, of course, volunteering for food. "What's for dessert?"

We were moving in the right direction, clearly, but continuing along an unknown path. I'm not good at uncertainty. I'm not brave about ambiguity.

I GOT LUCKY IN MANY WAYS that fall. If you plug "anorexia" into any search engine, guide to periodical literature, Medscape database, or newsgroup listing you fall back from the huge volume of hits. "Anorexia" as a keyword will net you everything from knock-knock jokes to pornography. It takes a lot of patience, slogging, and experience to get a sense of what out there is useful and what is not. Early in the search I would get very teary and sometimes even dizzy: after all, this was my child, a normal healthy child whose most serious transgression to date was the time she left a glass of juice in her room for a week. The worst illness she'd needed me to research was a chronic sinus infection.

I discovered, surprisingly quickly, that much of what the popular literature of anorexia sells as truth is actually quite disputed. The gap between "the literature" and the ears and eyes of parents was wide and deep. What is well established among the professionals is something parents might like to know: too little is known.

I became a devoted fan of several researchers on the trail of anorexia's genetic roots. I followed their careers and work like they were celebrities. I Googled, I MEDLINEd, I subscribed to clipping services. I developed academic crushes and made a special place on my wall for quotes from their papers and media interviews.

"The evidence is slowly gathering," one of my favorites was quoted saying. "We know that this is not a disease caused by bad parenting."

My new favorite scholar responded to my international fan mail within forty-eight hours. Dr. N. shared some research, gave me some papers to read, and treated me with compassion and respect. And he said something that cheered me immensely: "There will be an answer to this within the next five years and it is important your daughter survives and is not damaged by starvation in the meantime."

24

FROM EARTHNIK TO PUSHER

I CANNOT SAY, IPSO FACTO, that the cause of anorexia is biochemical so let's fire up the Bunsen burner and kill that thing. Getting a diagnosis is not the same as knowing how to cure a disease, but good science depends on focusing the research in the right direction and collecting the pertinent data. The longer we waffle and obfuscate about the cause of eating disorders, the longer it will take to find effective therapies.

Besides, I'm a flower child of the '60s. I believe in a glass of water for headaches, natural childbirth, and a mother's kisses for boo-boos. I just say no to Tylenol and I resist antibiotics. I was not ready to give Olympia the little pink pills until I saw a desperation in her face that required a relief I had no home cure for. The antidepressants did not in the end seem to change her essential nature in any way, they just softened an intolerable level of anxiety. But in the end I would not have begrudged them some small side effect if they saved her life and her bright future. I am a hippie girl, but with a scientific nature. And I am a mother.

Early on, I asked our pediatrician for some relief for Olympia's emotional misery and received a sample packet and a prescription that sat for a month on my desk while she refused to take it and we refused to beg her. Anorexics are rarely prescribed antidepressants because they depend on full nutrition to work. In our daughter's case, because the refeeding and the medicine were started around the same time, we may never know what role those pills played in the gradual resurfacing of her sanity and personality. We tapered off the drugs after a year and saw no quantifiable changes. Children are not guinea pigs to be experimented on, and even my scientific mind can stand not to know: we did what we could as quickly as we could with no regrets.

You do what you have to at the time, and you keep moving forward. Pharmaceuticals are not a panacea, but they have their place.

My reading revealed a possible zinc deficiency as well as other suspected nutritional insufficiencies that could play a role in anorexia, so it seemed obvious to provide a widely varied diet supplemented by multivitamins. Another pill by the breakfast plate.

I read about yogurt's beneficial effects on rebuilding the intestinal tract's flora arrangement, and we incorporated that into her diet daily. Deep green leafies supplied iron and B vitamins for depression. Bananas were for potassium. Water washed it all down.

I had a brief fling with the artificial sweetener Equal, which is a precursor to norepinephrine, because of an offhanded remark in an Australian newspaper. It required an extreme effort of acting to keep a straight face while feeding a calorie-free product to a child who is simultaneously consuming a quarter cup of butter. But no one said anorexia was for wimps. Eventually a representative of Equal's manufacturer, though thankful for my business, pointed out that the amount of active ingredient I was sprinkling over Olympia's smoothies was easily attainable in a small serving of meat or fish. We went back to sugar and added more meat.

Somewhere along the line I started feeding our entire family fish oil and flaxseed oil. They laugh about it but dutifully take them every evening. Elijah thinks my little bowl of caplets and gelcaps and Superhero vitamins at the dinner table is great fun. I just picture the little pink and grey neurons of my children drinking it all in and smile.

But mostly, the drug of choice was food. We ate and ate and ate and ate. What criminals.

I must tell you how incredulous I am, even now, that most anorexics must be hospitalized before the most simple and effective treatment known to science for eating disorders is administered: three square meals a day.

25

NIGHT AND DAY

YOU MAY NOT BE TOLD TO BLAME yourself directly. They'll let you point
your own finger of blame. When you ask a psychiatrist whether you did
this to your child, she will not tell you yes or no. You can sit in family
therapy and listen to your child attack your parenting style or your vanity or your marriage, but don't expect the therapist to step in to defend
you. You'll catch on, eventually. You'll hear the other parents obsessing
on how they didn't listen enough, or worked too many hours, or let
someone abuse their child.

You will pay the bills, follow instructions, and keep silent.

The guilt is self-serve, unlimited hours. And no one is going to stop
you.

If you deny it—defend your life, your parenting, your child's former
sanity—you will usually just get a blank stare. It is a parent's calling to
take the blame.

You will notice a new muddy mantra in the eating disorder discussion. Instead of addressing or debunking the family dysfunction model
of eating disorder origin, we hear that "it is not helpful" to dwell on who
is to blame.

I'll tell you what. It is "not helpful" to hear this. It is sly—a wink and a condescending nod. We parents get it. "Don't dwell on it, you'll just make it worse. Come on your penitent knees and behave. We won't yell at you any more."

This is not a position from which parents should operate. It is a position to suffer silently in, because we will blame ourselves, obviously, and we think we deserve it. From this position we cannot do the work, the hard work, of supporting our ill child, the one that the paid professionals will release to us when our insurance or our home equity lines run out. They will not be there. We will.

If you are a loving, healthy parent or loved one—and you know who you are—don't let yourself or anyone else blame you and make you think you should leave your child to her disease and to someone else's care. Your flaws are no greater the day after the diagnosis than the day before. Be who you are, support your child, and don't give up. It is your business.

LIKE ANY PARENT, I BLAMED MYSELF. I faced myself squarely and took full responsibility for all the faults I could find. But responsibility also means having the bravery to stand up and say when the emperor has fewer clothes than we're told. We stood up for our family and for our daughter, and I do not apologize for that.

I stand up now for other parents. I stand up for their right to have supportive coaching to help their children who have eating disorders long before those children need hospitalization. I stand up for their right to be a healthy part of their children's recovery—and to not be suspected criminals. I stand up for an end to game-playing and triangulation with therapists. I stand up for parents being parents, which is what we do best.

We finally found that kind of support. William Nuit is not an eating disorder specialist. He is not part of any treatment team. He doesn't even entirely agree with Samuel and me on the etiology of Olympia's anorexia. But he believes in us. We found him in an unlikely way—he had been our trusted marriage counselor years before, so we went to him to ask his recommendations for finding an eating disorder specialist and getting support for our family. Over the course of the conversation we decided to try a new idea. We went to Olympia to ask if she would meet with William.

"It is my job," William said, "to gain her trust."

He had ours.

He would see Olympia in private sessions, and the family every few months, with the goal of supporting her and coaching us through her recovery. As a family we set the terms and our goals. No secrets. No nonsense. This is what we needed all along—a family coach and sounding board. He believes in open communication, unconditional love, and imperfect parents. He believes in her. It is mutual.

26

LIFE SUPPORT—NO, NOT THAT KIND

MY FIRST INSTINCT, ON FALLING DOWN the rabbit hole, was to cover my face and unlist my phone number. Although I had not yet been formally educated on the etiquette of parenting an anorexic, I had absorbed enough of the local language to know I should feel a bit hurt, a bit angry, and a whole lot ashamed.

I still, at first, lived the outward life of the mother of the "good kid" and still basked in the blushing favor of my envious friends. I never took credit, exactly, for Olympia's poise, intelligence, and good nature, but I didn't mind standing next to her.

In my new life of emotional exile from normalcy, however, I sought out other parents of disordered eaters. I knew they would be my best bet for finding information, if not comfort. First I inventoried my mind and address book for parents I already knew who might have a clue what this was about. I came up blank. I could think of no one in my present or past life—since a girl in high school—who had mentioned an eating disorder. Not in college, not at work. None of my friends, none of my daughter's friends.

There are three possible explanations for this. One, eating disorders are rare and I've just missed knowing anyone touched by them. Two, this is the kind of secret you just don't mention to anyone. Or three, I wasn't listening. Knowing myself, I'm guessing a combination of these are true. I think eating disorders have happened near me but I didn't know. Like most people, I am self-centered and don't notice what goes on around me until and unless it touches me.

I tried telling a few close friends, hoping they'd point me to others. No luck. What looked to me like pity and helplessness and the glimmer of "Well, I've always thought . . ." put that experiment to rest.

I accosted a few parents in the waiting room of Joy's office. They backed away like I was John Brown recruiting conspirators.

I found no parent support groups in our area, nor even any support groups for sufferers. Even though we live within an hour of Washington, D.C., we found no public listings for support groups. This experience is not uncommon, I've discovered. You'd think there would be a support group for everything out there—from mothers of multiples to colostomy patients—but for the parents of 1–7 percent of the population, there is no meeting at the local Y.

So I went online.

Most of the discussion groups I stumbled on were for sufferers. The ones for parents were not very active. They mostly consisted of sorrowful cries into the ether begging for help.

One site was entirely different. Samuel found it and insisted I join. He and I took on user names and dove into the "somethingfishy" site, so named because "scales are for fish." The site (for sufferers, families, and others) is unique in both its level of activity and its sense of community. There we found an established and active group of parents, mostly mothers, struggling with the same problems and issues as we were. Online I found parents who also knew mealtimes as minefields and who shared with us that mixture of terror and hope that was our new lifestyle. Instead of doomed cries of anguish, I found reasoned and information-filled conversations. Real support was offered by real people. After an initial sense of disbelief and grief that we had anything in common with such suffering, I felt both accepted and relieved. I eagerly joined in the support, the questions, and the banter.

Samuel and I began to speak of the different people online as though they were neighbors or coworkers.

"Who are you talking about?" Olympia occasionally asked.

"Friends."

"You know, you shouldn't make 'friends' on the Internet," she laughed. "My parents taught me that."

Samuel lacked patience when the discussions turned to "feelings" and endlessly supportive threads of "me, too." He sought information and debate. For me it was a welcome emotional connection and I was moved and engaged by the personalities and the ongoing stories of families like ours. Samuel wanted data. I craved contact. There, I felt less alone.

Eventually it became more important to me to check on the last hour's messages than to read my "real" e-mail or hear my real phone messages. I kept a list of posters, their stories, their children's ages and diagnoses, and their real names—when given. I used my pseudonym, as most there do, but the experience still felt real and so did the Jane123s and the Scaredmoms.

WHICH MADE IT ALL THE MORE PAINFUL when Samuel and I went from participants to pariahs.

I learned quickly that the Maudsley approach was unknown to the families on the board. When I enthusiastically posted articles advocating the approach, other parents put me in my place by calling such approaches "controversial" and "coercive." I continued to mention the method to any new parent arriving on the board asking "How can I get my child to eat?" and "What can I do?"

For those who arrived asking, "What did I do wrong?" I posted articles and data about biological causes of anorexia and information that countered blame-based assumptions about eating disorders.

The idea that parents could or should support their children in eating was attacked. Most of the parents believed it must be left to the therapists and the children to decide when and what to eat. Eating with your anorexic, it became clear, was in poor taste. Nearly every single parent on the board had a reason why they had contributed to or caused their child's illness. When I stated I did not, I could almost hear the gasps through my modem.

Samuel took a more direct approach, posting fat-filled tips on ways for parents to feed their children. These posts caused a flurry of indignant responses. Parents were incredulous that he would talk about food at all, not to mention fattening food.

"I feel sorry for your daughter," said one.

It took a while, but at some point I realized I was no longer getting much out of the experience. Samuel had already stopped posting. I no longer felt free to ask questions or seek comfort, because my inquiries had become an invitation to question our methods. I felt very much misunderstood and spent a lot of time composing my responses, gathering data to share. I realized that what our family was doing was antithetical to much of what is taught and practiced with American families. I lost the feeling that I was with kindred spirits. My attendance trailed off.

Finally one of my posts, a strident one, was "locked" and deleted by the owners.

"You can't save the world," a friend told me.

But I felt as though I had been exiled from my lunch table at school.

I LOOKED FOR SUPPORT FOR OLYMPIA, TOO. I found a raging debate there, as well.

Support groups for sufferers, I learned, face the evil twins of competition and self-delusion. Sufferers compete to see who is sickest and often brag about their failed attempts to change. Support groups of young people with eating disorders are notorious for becoming tutorials on hitherto unthought-of behaviors. So are treatment centers. At one office we visited, the teenage participants were closely monitored in the hallway to keep them from sharing contact information.

I know many people who say such groups are the only way to get through to a sufferer on his or her own level. They argue that no one who does not suffer in this way can possibly understand or see through the self-deceptions. But I can't stop wondering: if the support group were for people who see little green men in their bathtubs, would it be better to discuss the specific shade of green or to address what diet and medications would reduce these delusions?

In the end this was one thing Joy and I agreed on—no support groups for a young anorexic. I would have balked if Olympia had started visiting websites or found her own group. It was better, in my mind, that she be less, rather than more, exposed to people with eating disorders. At an AA meeting I know there would be no booze. At an anorexic group I am guessing there is no food.

MY DAUGHTER DID ENCOUNTER other classmates with eating disorders, but except for one, she did not reach out to them.

I don't know if that was good or bad. I worried about her lack of peer support. I worried about her privacy and her reputation. I wondered whether unknowingly the people in her life would enable her or wound her. I thought it would be better if she did not have something to hide and suggested that she not keep it a secret.

"People think of anorexics as freaks, Mom. It's a joke to them."

I have not yet lived long enough to forget the primacy of high school social relations. The weight of recovery was great enough; saving the world, or even educating one small high school, was far too much to ask. She was ill, and then she recovered, in private.

Of course, we had the luxury of privacy because we cared for her at home and she stayed in school. For families whose children are inpatients at hospitals or at residential centers, there is no secret to keep. Friends, neighbors, and classmates all know they've left and when they've returned. The issue is on the table. Some families find they receive unexpected support from their communities. I have heard of schools that made safe accommodations, employers who helped a parent be there for a child's meals, and neighbors who kept an eye out for recovering anorexics. I was glad to learn that being public can open up support, not just the disapproval and voyeurism we dread.

I FOUND MY OWN SUPPORT among my close friends and family. Instead of only allowing ourselves the company of those who agreed with us, I made it a point to teach the people around us about what we were doing and why. But it was lonely. It still is.

Was I brave? No. Just scared. You are bathed in fear all day until you can hear it like a sound. Your dreams are ugly and nervous. There is no rest, no respite from fear. You don't know what will happen, or when. There is so little to do but watch your life slow to the vibration of intimate fear.

My friends kept me alive that year of fear. Aside from my husband, my heroic partner, I was preserved by friendship.

Jayne was ever practical, letting me download my thoughts without editing them, although in real life she was my editor. She never showed any doubt about the decisions we made. She closely observed each of us in the family, monitoring us and stepping in when needed.

Ro sat on my porch that first week and let me cry and be hateful and terrified for hours.

Maura lent me her RV when I was ready to get away and write this all down.

Bette gave me a field to camp in, a horse to ride, and a sunset with a beer.

My mother, who in adulthood is also my friend, grounded me with her incredible and unconditional love for Olympia and the rest of us.

Cass pressured me into an exercise class that, once a week, made me take care of my body and suffer along with others in mutual health.

Tina, who knew, cried for me fiercely, without pity.

Carlina, who did not know, gave me unpaid advice about myself and about life in general that was better than any I paid for. It mostly involved laughing.

Joanna and Ariane gave me the tremendous gift of not asking, specifically, what was wrong. And they did not abandon me, either, as most of the people I did not burden with my secret did. Telling them would have meant making them keep a secret from other mutual friends and acquaintances, but I wished I could. I thought they might understand if I did. I'll never know what kind of friendship we could have had.

Friends, that year, became people I could tell. My heart was too bruised to be with anyone I had not. I'm terrible at secrets.

If Olympia had had cancer there would have been no question about telling others. A leukemia diagnosis would have been awful, but we would not have kept it to ourselves. My neighbors might have brought casseroles. Other friends might have checked in on me, helped with babysitting, made me go out to lunch with them, fed Olympia. I would not have avoided conversations in public places, would not have hated talking to people, would not have made excuses for why I was not doing something or was doing something. When my daughter went into remission, as she so wonderfully now has, people would have said how happy they are for me.

They would have patted Olympia on the back and complimented her for her bravery and for how well she seems now. They would perhaps have shared their own stories of loss and healing with her in a way that would have helped her. She might have been able to talk to others who were struggling—and felt better herself.

That year, if it had been cancer, I might have felt strong instead of strident, brave instead of secretive, scared but not alone.

BUT WHEN I FELT ALONE, I turned to books, a common refuge of mothers like me. To teach ourselves, to fill in some of the spaces between what our children's caregivers tell us and what we observe, we read. We look for literature to help us reason with our children, to inspire us, to give to our bewildered friends.

But the books we bring home sometimes end up in the hands of anorexics early in their illness. They are notoriously poor listeners, filtering their materials through the current state of their mental health. The ill read the memoirs of anorexics and bulimics and instead of fear they find inspiration. Some anorexics call these tales of extreme woe "bibles" and use them to gather tips on better living through starvation.

We parents buy the self-help books and the "I survived" books looking for answers, but we mostly find muddy theories that throw in a bit of everything that has ever been said or believed about eating disorders, regardless of their incompatibility or of more recent evidence discrediting them. Much of what we read tells us to back away. The secret language of eating disorder books is generally: be quiet, know your place. The people buying and reading most of the books are parents—mothers primarily—so it is ironic that it is those mothers who find themselves so ill-used.

AND WHEN ALL ELSE FAILED, my exhausted eyes took refuge in trees.

"They are not under- or overweight. Nothing about them is more or less or troubling." (My journal, October 2, 2002.)

The trees are still there. So are we.

27

THE SIRENS

I'm going to tell you something scary. Now that you know how dangerous and insidious this disease is, you will be depressed to learn that there are those who actually promote the illness. The Internet has provided the opportunity for very sick people, and I mean that literally, to promulgate the idea that anorexia is "a lifestyle choice."

On their websites you can read the personification of the disease. Some sufferers give it a name (often a variant of Anna or Ed), and write letters to it as if to a lover. You can read pseudopolitical manifestos on "free will" and diatribes against fascist parents, authority figures, and people who eat.

Anorexics, more than bulimics and binge eaters, often become very competitive. My daughter, on learning about a support group for anorexics, recoiled in horror: "I'm way too big. They'd laugh at me." She was at her lowest weight at that time and couldn't sit still for long because her lack of padding cut off her circulation.

Perhaps this competitive orientation is caused by the illusion of discipline that is involved with self-starvation. The world conspires to validate the ill person through compliments and envious comments. I'm sure Aztec virgins got a lot of "atta girls" on their way up the steps as well. Perhaps the distorted sense of reward stems from the torture of having no respite or relief in the cycle of disease; after all, bulimics get to eat and then purge, and binge eaters have their brief moment of release as they eat.

I don't want you to have to experience one of these pro-anorexia sites, so I hope you appreciate the difficulty I had in experiencing the following for you:

One particularly vile site generously lets anorexics post pictures of themselves. Prefaced by "my pics, bleh" and "my fat photo," girls compete for your attention. They want you to look at their "uglee fat" selves and their skull-faces.

Another generous site offers "thinspiration" to brighten your day with "tons of celebrity and model pics," as well as calculators to determine your anemic body mass index and "master cleanser" recipes to clean out your system: of food. Ever supportive of your right to die, you can find empowering and supportive sites that glorify the art of near death.

Scared yet?

The author of one site is utterly without illusions. She warns away mere dieters and people who are still new enough to their disorder to get out. The "tips" section is not for sissies: eat nonfat foods because they taste awful and will help you not eat; sleep a lot; put pictures of things that make you sick next to your meal, or photos of models; sabotage your food with too much salt or pepper; shower when you feel hungry—you won't want to dirty yourself with food. She doesn't advise purging, but offers these kind hints if you do: hydrate before using laxatives, and eat things in reverse order to what you want to keep in your system. For those who are new to the secrecy of the craft, she offers this: have a socially acceptable "diet" to discuss; continue to buy food, but throw it away; and this gem: "Don't deny everything if confronted. People will believe a little truth with a big lie much easier than a huge lie. Act as if it's no big deal instead of reacting emotionally and people will tend to believe you."

You are not going to get the addresses for these websites out of me, though, for three reasons. The obvious one is that they sicken and sadden me and although I'm not an advocate of censorship I don't think these tortured monsters need the extra hits. Another reason is that these sites change addresses a lot. The webmasters for these sites complain bitterly about discrimination and rail against the movement out there to ban them. Internet providers are under pressure to disallow them, and many have complied. Last, your anorexic does not need to find you surfing that ugly part of the Net.

Nevertheless, these sites are innumerable and readily accessible to anyone with an Internet connection. The anarchic nature of the Internet prevails.

I have corresponded with some of these people, who call themselves Pro-Anas. They believe themselves to be higher beings, possessing self-control that the rest of us mortals lack. They trade tips and encourage each other. They would seem to the uninitiated—if their cause was to ban music censorship or to end all wars—like passionate and normal teenagers.

We amuse anorexics. They laugh at us. We are hypocrites, slovenly undisciplined fakers who have no place moralizing, lecturing, and tut-tutting under our breath.

It is a good world for anorexics. A world of solitary eating, diet slavery, and the necessity of devising, every single one of us individually, a unique routine of meals, cuisine, and quantity.

AT THE HEIGHT OF MY DAUGHTER'S ILLNESS, when I could see that she was so desperately driven by the need to avoid food that she would deceive me, I feared those pro-anorexia sites. I feared the tricks and the tips, but most of all I feared the validation. To a mind seeking relief from an agony of anxiety, such websites must be a perfect prescription. I feared any intimations from the outside world that might undermine the reality that we wanted her to see: that eating was necessary, healthy, and good. That her anorexia was an illusion, a mirage.

I'm sad to say that the entrenched anorexics I have encountered online and in first-person accounts have been decidedly unpleasant people. They remind me of some people I know who are crippled by a life lived under real and suspected bigotry. Sometimes things are not your fault, but they can make you ugly nonetheless.

Olympia once referred to the anorexia as "part of me" and said she could not take sides. I can. I love my daughter. I hated her anorexia. A few weeks into her starvation, my daughter begged me to leave her be. "I'm happy now," she said. But she was crying.

For those who suffer long with the active disease, the person and the illness seem to become irretrievably entwined. As much as I intellectually believe those with eating disorders to be people compelled by involuntary urges and as well as I know them to be backed into a corner, I find I dislike them intensely. I'm sorry.

28

"YOU'RE NOT FAT!"

THERE ARE DIFFERENT WAYS to say it.

"*You're* not fat!" really means, "My dear, listen to me, you are not the one with a problem. *You* are beautiful—skinny, thin, trim, slim, svelte, all those good things. Look around you at all the really fat people. They are disgusting. *You're* not like that. *You're* just right. *You* are fine. *You* have got it right; you're killing yourself for nothing. Don't worry, *you* are not one of us fat, lumpy, corpulent things. *You* are thin, perfect, wonderful, virtuous. Honey, stop this anorexia thing because you don't need to worry: thin is good and you *are* thin. Thin, thin, thin!"

Then there's "You're *not* fat!" which is an ongoing and futile argument that you cannot win. You start out patient but end up bitter. With this tactic you argue against all the ways your anorexic insists there is something wrong with her. This is anorexia as an affront. Anorexia as an insult to the rest of us. Anorexia as arrogance and snobbery and manipulation. As overachievement and a plea for attention. "You're *not* fat" is how we tell our anorexic to drop it, cut it out, give it up, and snap out of it. You're *not* fat, but you are annoying, you are tedious, you are exhausting.

"You're not *fat!*" is another animal entirely. You're not *fat*, but you are abused, confused, and my "cause of the week." You are not *fat*, you are the embodiment of my political causes, my unified theory on why the world is going to pieces. You are not *fat*, but you are *full* of potential to prove me right about what is wrong in the world and about my plan to cure everything. You are a vessel, a platter, an icon. You've been neglected and damaged but I'll save you. It isn't about the food, darling. You're not *fat*, you are afraid of taking up space. You are not *fat*, you are fragile. You are afraid of getting old, having sex, making decisions. Let me replace your fear of fat with a fear of men, of love, of risk, of life. You're not *fat*.

"But you're not fat," you want to say. It almost escapes your lips. Others—grandparents, annoyed classmates, disoriented in-laws—cannot keep it in. Why not?

Is being overweight such a sin? You would think that the fear of being fat is such a powerful idea that we actually think it rational to "diet" to the point of death. If it is rational, we think, we can talk them out of it.

We are all bizarrely participatory in the eating disorder when we grimly insist on weight gain as a barometer of wellness. We assess weight gain in the anorexic as though it were a measure of recovery from the disease. Lacking a skin test or titer we gather around the scale as if it could tell us what goes on in the mind. But the mind is where it hurts.

Of course eating disorders are not about the food. But we still tell the anorexics, the bulimics, the binge eaters that their weight—our perception of their ideal weight—is a measure of their disease. And we insist, as if it matters deeply, that "you are not fat." Small wonder they don't think we understand.

"Be *fat*" is what the anorexic thinks you're saying when you say "eat." So I guess fat is good. Fat must mean healthy and stable. Fat must be alive.

"Be fat, honey." Be big and glorious and alive. Do not live on a margin between anorexic and anorexic plus half a pound. Be alive, really alive, be somewhere where the scale can't find you, somewhere where the scale means nothing. Be whatever your body wants to be when it is satisfied after every meal, when it walks with a bounce, when it can dance when no one's looking. And even when they are.

Yes! Go ahead. Be fat!

29

RESHELVING

OLYMPIA ASKED ME ONCE, six months after she first became ill, whether she was still the same person she had been before.

"Of course you are, honey!" I tried to reassure her with a list of things that she used to do and love. Choking back all the things that involved food, I had to change the subject. There were too few. You cannot separate life from food. None of us can.

Not long after that question, she thoroughly cleaned her room. She put five bags of trash outside her room. In the bags were perhaps a third of the magazines in her room. The family cookbooks reappeared in the kitchen. Food no longer ruled her life.

I was relieved, but wondered whether she was now less than she had been or whether something had come to fill in the space?

During her illness, I kept a diary addressed to her because I had so much I wanted to tell her. Every morning I spilled out the things that gave me hope, the new things I had learned, the way she had faced some new challenge. It was a time capsule, a bottled message I hoped she would someday find, but one I hoped she would never need.

Every week, my entries got shorter. Every month, it seemed, there was less that couldn't be said.

Olympia's mind came back incrementally. It was one bite at a time. As far as she was concerned, her illness went from "not anorexia" to "a problem I have with eating" to "when I was anorexic." It was gradual, like watching a season change. It was satisfying, like a dreaded flood receding.

Her health returned steadily, but she struggled with her mind. She experienced fear, relief, annoyance, anger, and occasionally fierce pride. Often, starving herself was still like a bad boyfriend: she was both attracted and repelled. She was ashamed of that attraction, but frightened not to give in. Yet as we let go, she usually stepped forward. She began to take charge of her own eating.

We had to stop counting her calories under our breath. No more weighing. No panic when she said she wasn't hungry. No strain in our voices when we asked, "Are you hungry?"

She backslid occasionally. There was a day out with friends where no one else seemed to want to stop to eat. One time she "forgot" to eat lunch until it was time for dinner. Her female friends never seemed, to her, to care about what time it was or how long it had been between meals. But Olympia was like a diabetic between injections, always aware of breakfast, lunch, dinner, snacks. Boys, she noticed, were without such compunctions. They ate volumes, frequently, happily.

"How do you know you are hungry?" She would ask. "How do you stop when you are full?"

When she faltered, we gave her a hug and assured her there was no shame in it. And we sat back down to eat. It was easier now to remain calm. We were familiar with the vocabulary of reassurance, of firm support, of no compromise. And she would rejoin us, resolute, and eat healthily again. Eating was normal, eating was good. We ate.

She had anorexia, but it didn't own her. Our anorexic became a person who had anorexia but was not defined by it. She was no longer a victim or a sufferer but a person with a disease—and a great laugh, a favorite TV show, a new hair style every morning, an A in precalculus, a dislike for zealots, a weakness for athletes, a flair for classic clothes, and a personality replete with things that had nothing to do with anorexia.

Anorexia lost its stranglehold on our emotions. We could laugh for other reasons than comic relief. We could eventually joke, even about the illness, and even with her. We called gymnastic competitions and beauty contests on TV "The Anorexia Channel." Instead of freezing in horror when we heard diet commercials, we shook our heads knowingly and smiled. The world was still crazy, but that was OK.

Once when Samuel professed a weakness for pie, Olympia suggested anorexia as a weight loss plan. And it seemed funny, because anorexia was no longer the dreaded bogeyman of our lives. It was a disease, one our daughter was beating with a healthy lifestyle and a medicine— food—that was available everywhere. And we were all on the same side.

30

STUFF AND RELEASE

I am not, strictly speaking, a Maudsleyan.

But a friend is. Martina reminds me that there really is no "Maudsley approach," according to the eating disorder specialists at Maudsley Hospital. As a recipient of the National Health Services of the United Kingdom, she should know.

Martina's daughter was fourteen when she became anorexic. As a British citizen, she was entitled to free health care and a share of whatever services were available. For eating disorders, that care is home- and family-based.

Her mother and I debate the American and the British systems.

I say, "At least you didn't have to pay for it!"

Martina says, "At least you were able to choose who to see."

"Martina, your country has an enlightened system that does not treat eating disorders as family dysfunctions!"

"Laura, you know very well the Maudsley approach is agnostic on causes."

"But Martina, at least you were treated as a family!"

"Badly. Incompetently at times. And in the end we did not follow their instructions well and my husband never thought much of it all. In fact, he hardly participated."

"Martina, I believe if American parents were given support they could care for their sick kids at home."

"And if British families were offered the opportunity to send their children inpatient they probably would!"

"But, Martina, it worked."

"But, Laura, your system works for plenty of people as well."

I KNOW THERE IS NO MAGIC PILL, no "answer."

There are, however, some things that are wrong. Some old, rotted, unusable ideas that deserve retirement, like considering eating a choice. Like punishing those with eating disorders for their behaviors. Like the idea of a "minimum weight."

And there are some good things out there, too. Like early detection. Like a zero-tolerance attitude toward malnutrition. Like parental involvement and supportive coaching for families. Like less hospitalization and more outpatient programs for eating disorders. Like more evidence-based treatment. Like respect and compassion, not pity, for those with eating disorders.

We can all agree on better informed doctors, coaches, peers, and media. We can collectively support public awareness on mental health issues. We can eat together more, diet less, and support each other more.

Perhaps the most important thing about the Maudsley approach is what it doesn't do, and how its successes reflect on previous approaches. It does not separate ill people from their lives and their natural support systems. It puts full nutrition first. And it is not based on the idea of family dysfunction or any particular dysfunction at all.

Our family didn't change the way we do things because the way we were before made her ill. We changed because it helped her get better.

But just because we did not break our anorexic does not mean we were perfect to start with. No one is. Life after anorexia can be better than before. I'll never be thankful for Olympia's illness, but I sure am proud of our family for facing it.

31

WHAT'S A NICE
THERAPIST LIKE YOU . . .

WHO ON EARTH WOULD WANT to treat anorexics? It has a low "cure" rate. Ill patients are almost always in denial, they relapse, they lie—and they die. What kind of therapist would want to take them on? Fellow anorexics, I learned, for a start.

You may or may not be surprised to know how many in the eating disorder treatment "community" have had eating disorders. It is a common selling point. Many therapists advertise for patients on the basis of their personal understanding of the disease. Many treatment centers boast about the recovered members of their staff. They claim they know the mind-set and the disease best, as well as how to treat it. They have a personal interest. But that rubs both ways.

Eating disorder care today is mostly administered by professionals trained in an earlier era, who are often themselves veterans of treatment in a time when family dysfunction was routinely blamed for eating disorders. The detritus of countless theories—many discredited or antiquated—lives on in the practices of therapists. They may promise to expunge traumatic "unmet needs" and "attachment disorders" with craniosacral/polarity therapy or to apply an "addiction model" to cope with "taking up space in a sometimes dangerous world." There are those who will help your anorexic recover a lost "connection with his or her true inner spirit." There are charlatans and incompetents and well-meaning fools, but from outside the therapy room it can be hard to tell the difference between help and the potential for grave harm.

All the eating disorder treatment available to our family was of the old school, and I believe it would have left our daughter sicker. Our daughter did not, after the initial period, starve while her loved ones watched helplessly. Olympia was not fed, in lieu of food, rationalizations for her "choice" of anorexic behaviors. She was not isolated from her loved ones and surrounded by other irrational and distressed people. She recovered from her illness in her own home, slept in her own bed, and went about most of the normal business of teenage life. She could be the face of a new type of recovery.

WE DO NOT KNOW what would have happened if our daughter had continued with traditional therapy. We do not even know what did happen in her therapy. When the therapy was terminated, our daughter's therapist, Joy, would not provide a written report on anything: no diagnosis or treatment goals, no results or recommendations. The therapy existed only in the room in which it transpired and in my daughter's memory. The only way to get copies of a therapist's notes—even of your own therapy—is through a court order. There is no way to quantify or dispute the results. No way, before or during, to really know what your child is learning in that room. The parent of a minor child in therapy, in the end, is just the chauffeur.

As parents, we don't just "want to be included." We are. We were there before, we are there throughout, and we are there afterward. Treat our children and you are treating us. Parents new to eating-disorder–land are generally not told that separation from the family, either physical or emotional, is nearly universal in the treatment of eating disorders. I thought it was just me. I dare say most of us do. But balanced with her responsibility to her client, a therapist has a responsibility to a licensing board, to a code of ethics, to insurers, and to the law. Parents are the least of her worries.

Helen Gremillion, a researcher who spent time in a major treatment center a few years back, described in her book, "Feeding Anorexia," the relationship between doctors, staff, and patient as a "surrogate family." The doctors serve as father figures, the staff (usually female) as mother figures, and the patients as the children. Parents, allowed to visit or even call only under limited circumstances, were infantilized in this relationship as well.

We, as parents, are not trusted. I can only conclude that we are excluded from the care and treatment of these grave illnesses because families are held responsible in the first place and because as nonprofessionals we are not considered competent. But loved ones, coached and supported by sound and professional guidance, should be an asset to the patient's treatment. Even hospitalized, an ill person has the right to closeness with her family; any system that denies that relationship as a matter of course needs to be questioned. Daddy may not know best, but he can learn.

As a parent, I believe that the removal of my daughter from her life and our home is a massive loss to both child and family, which cannot but weaken everyone. For an appendectomy, I am advised to never leave my child alone in the hospital, to double-check pharmacy doses, to keep an eye on the IV drip. But at a time of critical emotional and physical need, we send ill young people away to closed wards and restricted phone calls.

"What—do you want to scrub for surgery as well, ma'am?" Maybe. If surgeons didn't have to account for their results and operated in secrecy with poor results, maybe we should ask if they washed their hands first.

There are times when the person with the eating disorder is too ill to be cared for at home. Eating disorders often coexist with depression, obsessive-compulsive disorders, self-inflicted harm, and suicidal behaviors. There need to be safe havens for these patients to be stabilized and observed. There are also families too toxic or too codependent or with too few resources to care for ill people in their homes.

The question is: how many ill people could be treated earlier and better to avoid the need for crisis care? With support, families might be able to avoid inpatient or residential care. Because most of the literature on eating disorders advises parents to back off, I can only wonder how many of us would do more—earlier and more effectively—if we knew how. If we were trusted with the tools and the authority, we could be there for our loved ones during their illness as we will be when they are well.

And if the worst happens and we must send our children to others' care, the ties to home should not be severed. Protect the sufferer for us, not from us.

I admire the practitioners who overcame their illnesses and dedicated themselves to helping others. I am in awe of those who have healed from eating disorders as well as from abuse, trauma, social pressures, and neglect. But it is time to retire some of the old thinking. People who have eating disorders deserve the benefit of contemporary knowledge about the brain. And their families deserve the benefit of the doubt, period.

32

SHOWING OUR COLORS

My family does not fit the profile of "premorbid dysfunction" that the experts tried to cram us into. We don't look the part and we don't act the part.

We're not alone. And it is time for the regular parents to step up and be counted. Time for the messy, loving, benignly neglectful, neither rich nor poor, ethnically diverse, and perfectly normal families to come forward. Our kids get eating disorders, too.

It turns out that anorexia is not about thinness and pressures and sex. It's not even about being an American.

Anorexia is found in China, Romania, the Caribbean. It is found among the Omani, whose women wear veils in public. There is evidence of bulimia in ancient Rome, and eating disorders were epidemic during the Renaissance. One young Dark Ages noblewoman's anorexia led to her canonization as a saint. People have been diagnosed with anorexia from ages five to ninety. Rich people get it, and poor families face it. Boy Scouts and tomboys and science-fair prizewinners alike are afflicted with it. The literature of anorexia is stuffed with the abused, the neglected, and the horribly damaged, but a lack of those tragedies does not provide protection. Too many nice things and a private school education don't give you anorexia; neither does not having them.

We count anorexics as those who end up on an eating disorder ward (or on "Entertainment Tonight"), but there are reasons to doubt that. Let us count the ways: patient denial, secrecy, distrust of psychiatry, a shortage of child psychiatrists, the loose network of therapists who advertise treatment of eating disorders, the lack of mandatory reporting, the flaccid nature of DSM diagnosis, comorbid conditions, social stigma, fear of losing insurance benefits, and financial concerns are only the most obvious barriers to good numbers. It is hard to count heads and even harder to quantify treatment results. Poorly understood, frankly, is the kindest thing I can say for the whole business. Thankfully, you don't have to take my word for it. The majority of professional eating disorder literature says the same thing.

Most people suffering from anorexia and other eating disorders are probably never identified. A study that compared diagnosis rates for identical patient charts with different attached photographs suggests that physicians are less likely to diagnose an eating disorder in a person who appears to be Hispanic or African-American than they would a "white" patient. An African-American friend of mine brought her underweight, nervous, fainting daughter to an ER and was pulled aside by the doctor: "Watch out for schizophrenia in this child." Not an eating disorder, schizophrenia. Wrong profile. Boys are less likely to be referred for an eating disorder and are most likely underdiagnosed. The elderly have their refusal to eat—the inability to eat—diagnosed as a separate disorder. People with eating disorders rarely volunteer for treatment, so they suffer—and sometimes die—in private and uncounted.

The modern stereotype of anorexia does not describe the disease; rather, it describes the demographics of those whose families seek and secure inpatient professional care. Although anorexia exists in all cultures, it is upper-middle-class Western white parents who are most likely to bring their daughters' problems to the attention of professionals.

These families are also the ones who are most likely to aggressively pursue care and to have health insurance to defray the considerable costs of therapy and hospitalization. By the time they get their children into treatment, these parents are almost as crazed as their children, thereby self-fulfilling the expected profile of overinvolved and overanxious parents.

Of course, not all the attention paid to upper-class women is misguided. Another thing all anorexics have in common is a diet. Kids on top of the social food chain are under more pressure to look the part, which at this point in history is thin. Since few people naturally grow up to be six feet tall and a size two, the rest turn to a diet. They stop eating. And for those with the genes to match, a diet is the key in the lock of an eating disorder.

While we dither about young, overindulged girls afraid of their breasts, anorexia nervosa is enjoying its run, picking off all kinds of people. Some die. For the longtime sufferers, the chronic food restriction over a lifetime cripples them with bone weakness and heart disease. Those who get off with just a scare also carry around an ugly lump of guilt and therapy-provided "reasons" they were ill.

Anorexics who survive and have children pass on their behaviors and their other coping mechanisms to their children with or without the genes to make them truly ill. This is another reason eating disorders are often blamed on moms—they usually share one or two bits of DNA with their children.

Successful anorexics influence other young people to emulate their illness, distorting the community's standards for healthy eating. Anorexia is not contagious, but disordered eating and the distorted body image that comes with the disease can have an impact on everyone the sufferer knows. Add that to the secrecy and shame common with eating disorders and you have a situation every bit as devastating as that experienced by the families of those who abuse drugs and alcohol or who have schizophrenia, bipolar disease, or borderline personality disorder.

I do not believe anorexia is an epidemic or a major threat to our nation's health. But I do know that our willfully pained and prurient vision of eating disorders says more about the rest of us than it does about those who suffer from them. We must know them to help them.

We need to update our mental snapshot of the anorexics among us and embrace the diversity of the sickness. We might help them as well as ourselves.

33

THEY ARE ILL. WHAT'S OUR EXCUSE?

ANOREXICS HAVE A DISEASE that makes them eat strangely, act irrationally, and see the world in a distorted way. But what are the rest of us thinking? So many of us eat according to insane fashions and on bizarre schedules. Many of us attribute moral judgments to where and on what and with whom we dine. Although none of us has actually met any of the airbrushed still-life apparitions in the magazines, we irrationally believe that it is actually each of us who is out of place. We feel shame, despite common sense, for the shape we take up, the height we grow, the shade we tan, and the pattern of our hair. We compulsively commit to and then quit exercise programs we have never done, do not like, and know very well we will not do. This is healthy?

But for our anorexics we reserve a special torture. We treat them as though they are sane.

It is their peculiar fate to fall victim to an illness that, instead of attacking their sense of balance or bringing on seizures, makes their own flesh seem alien to them. In a cruel coincidence, the world and era in which they live is currently wallowing in a seemingly similar malaise.

But it is not the same. Anorexics are not simply taking our craziness to an extreme or taking us too literally.

Yet we react to their starvation as though it were rational. We respond like maniacs to their illness, waving our arms and shrieking and wringing our hands. We beg, we plead, we bargain. We look to them to explain themselves, when it should be the rest of us explaining our actions and apologizing for setting such bizarre examples. We don't know how to act, what to do, whom to listen to. We send mixed messages, send them to conflicting professionals, and then send them off to find themselves.

The people we consult tell us to back off, and for some crazy reason we abdicate our parental roles, pretend to go on with our lives, and then throw up our hands in frustration when the nothing we keep doing doesn't work. Our ill children look to us for stability but we give in to their disease. We ask *them* "why are you doing this?" instead of telling them, and we tell *them* to be rational when we are not rational ourselves. We watch our loved ones starve or purge, and we suffer without catching them as they fall. Who are we calling disordered?

If we want our anorexics to follow the bread crumbs back to reality, we will have to find our way there, too. They look at our hysteria and think we are ill—and we need to prove them wrong.

Our family searched in vain for support in making our home and our behavior a safe haven for our child during her illness. Not to mention her school, her peer group, or even her doctor's office. We decided to offer safety, not coercion or anger. Safety from dangerous delusions, not from us. For this the professionals treated us with suspicion. We were made to feel like bad parents and led to question our own sanity and our qualifications to evaluate our child's care.

But even without professional support, a family can be a safe haven for loved ones reeling from the emotional and physical ravages of an eating disorder. We can provide a loving time out. To do that we must do something strange: eat. We must eat with our anorexics.

And we can keep looking until we find professionals who think we should.

34

HAPPY LIVING DAY

OLYMPIA ALWAYS LOVED A PARTY. She is like her mother (whose fortieth birthday lasted two weeks) and grandmother (who throws herself huge parties and invites everyone including her younger brother's former Cub Scout leader). Our family likes to celebrate milestones. They define the phases of a life and provide lines to step over to mark your progress.

One year had passed since the beginning of Olympia's illness. We had no party to mark it.

One year since a sports injury brought on a week in which Olympia ate little; when she did get back up she was dizzy. There were surgeons, uncertainty, fear, tensions, and then an overwhelming obsession with food.

Olympia was now back to karate, swim team, and track. She ran for junior class secretary and lost—and lived. She tried out for a school play, was not chosen, and survived. She had surgery on her knee and healed. She earned her Red Belt in tae kwon do. She enjoyed outings with friends, sports events, movies, and travel anywhere out of this small town. She had more friends and more activities than before. She took more risks, laughed more, was more thoughtful. She matured a lot over a tough twelve months.

She looked healthier. She appeared more relaxed and engaged than she ever did. Our family was closer than we were before, and, interestingly enough, happier.

Was it worth it? No.

None of us is the same. We no longer look at the future with unblemished optimism. We understand the risks of relapse and the necessity of building a strong support system for Olympia and for ourselves. We know ourselves to be vulnerable to a world we had formerly commandeered. Life seems impermanent, which of course it is.

I harbor the belief that Olympia's anorexia would have happened sooner or later, and that it is better that it happened now, at home. I believe it was triggered, physiologically, by the starvation of a very stressful week; once set in motion, the damage was difficult to repair. Its effects linger. I believe that the year of healing strengthened her in a way that will be protective throughout her life but that she will always be vulnerable to disturbances in her body chemistry from stress, illness, and low nutrition. As it is for any family that has survived grave illness, she knows we will never be able to not care about her health or to take everything at face value. It would be the same if she had had cancer.

At one year we still served Olympia most meals and she looked to us to support her eating and her choices. But perhaps it is not so strange. For most people in the world, food is not something you make many choices about. Most people get up in the morning and eat the same food their ancestors ate, served by someone in their family—someone not interested in whether they are avoiding carbs this week or on a shiitake kick. Dietary choices are the luxury—and bane—of modern American life. Perhaps this constant choosing and innovation and individual decision making is really more aberrant than freeing.

BUT, WHAT DID SHE LOOK LIKE, you want to know. You want—let's be frank—to get a good look at her.

I could describe how beautiful she is, how alive and whole and heroic. But you can form your own picture. It looks just like a child you know and love. Hold that image.

Another mother I know took out baby pictures when her daughter fell ill with bulimia. Mina displayed them prominently: "This is who we're fighting for, honey. This is who you are fighting for."

There are only one or two pictures of Olympia from that fall. One from behind at the beach the first week, which I took to show her that she was not "big" as she was insisting and I was still arguing. The other, also from behind, was of someone else—ostensibly—and shows only the hollow under her collar bone. I asked her, later, if she wanted to see them; she said no.

What does Olympia remember of that year? "Not much," she says.

How much do we adults remember of dreams, of hallucinations, of sleepless weeks or drunken evenings or madness? How much can a fifteen-year-old remember of fourteen? A year later she was finally able to share a snack off a communal plate or fix her own dinner. She talked about her body and mostly said she liked it. When she felt afraid, she talked about that, too. And we listened.

Olympia thought of the year as wasted. She was determined not to be ill again, because recovery was so painful. She actively worked to keep her thoughts rational and her actions consistent; she sought feedback. She remembers, but it is a sore place. Where her father and I saw only progress and recovery, she saw loss, waste, regret.

As parents, we were told the most chilling thing possible: "Your daughter may die." And as simply as that, we set aside things like whether our front lawn was fertilized, whether our twenty-fifth high school reunion invitation would find us, and whether we would grow old.

As a teenager with little sense of the past or the enormity of adulthood, Olympia was told something much worse than possible death. She was told she was different. Not unique or special or "most likely to." Sick.

Our family's approach was that it was not her fault, but she had a serious illness that could kill her and made everything she did and said suspect. This was not welcome news to a teenage girl who heretofore laid claim to normal and had her sights on "perfect." For her it might have been far better to hear that she had chosen to starve herself in an attempt to get our attention, to protest her rotten circumstances, and to take back control from a world gone crazy. She could have taken that and molded it into a sculpture of dignity, self-righteousness, and independence.

By blaming us, or teen culture, or the disappointment of her knee injury, she would have had a solid hook on which to hang the misery of illness and added some virtue to the bitterness of recovery. Instead, she was handed—by those who she knows to love her best—a diagnosis of biological illness that had broken her. I can only imagine how much she resented that. How much she probably always will.

We took over, not waiting for her to participate in her recovery, and for a long time she didn't even ask why. She resented the whole process, the sense of being tainted and ill, the gaining of weight, the guilt, and the psychological work of deconstructing the ideas that had formed like stalactites in her nutrient-starved brain. As she awakened, over months of low-stress, well-protected, fully fed living, she resented the fact that she had to heal at all. That these pernicious thoughts about her body, about food, about other people's motives, had not been hers alone, and therefore unique.

Although she had not broken her brain, she still had to go through herself and reboot all the synapses.

She is ambivalent about this book.

She is thankful, but not always.

Once, at a seaside table in Mexico with my mother, she spoke about it. She told my mother that Samuel and I had saved her life and that she could never repay us. And with that, she did. And no more is said.

"It is so internal," she once said.

"Do you mean deep inside or subconscious?" I asked, aware that these moments are rare and I must not startle her or be too intense.

"I mean inside yourself—only a little is visible."

I understood. The anorexia that we could see in her actions and health were nothing compared to the storm inside. And how scary it was. And why it is so hard to see—no blood test, no pH strip, no brain scan can expose it. She had no way to share it or give it away.

What do anorexics want? They want to eat, she says. They lie, cheat, rage, and scheme to avoid it—and feel proud of the discipline—but they want to eat. They are starving and they know it but they cannot give themselves permission to eat—some force tells them not to. Some inner voice, which becomes their friend, praises their discipline and whispers away the irrationality of it.

"It is like being in a club, almost. You understand what people are going through, the things they say about it," Olympia says of the anorexics and bulimics she hears on TV interviews.

"You get it," I said.

"Yeah."

"But it is bad, right?" My fears were showing.

"Yes, Mother," she sighed. "It is bad, but you see: I get it. And other people don't. No one understands that you can't just stop. You can't stop it. You know but you can't."

Her sympathy for others has grown, even as she has become more reserved, more careful. She watches carefully for signs of disordered eating in her friends. She refers, occasionally, to having "had a problem," if she thinks it would help someone. She knows things other people just cannot understand.

We never blamed her, but sometimes she blames herself.

She remembers being thinner, although she finally threw away the clothes that should never fit her again. She remembers a girl who asked with admiration how she got so thin. She remembers that no boys asked her out when she was sick.

She remembers being ill but sometimes beautiful.

She remembers being happy, in parts. Angry. And hungry.

So hungry.

AFTERWORD

THERE ARE TWO QUESTIONS that matter to parents faced with an eating disorder in their child: "Why?" and "What do we do now?" The questions are related.

The message that parents contribute to or outright cause eating disorders in their children is one that divides and destroys families. Parents given this message are thereafter crippled with guilt, shame, and helplessness just at the time their children may most need their support and strength. Generations of parents have absorbed this message and, out of love, relinquished their children's care to others.

Alternately, we are sometimes told that our ill children have chosen their illness, and it is their responsibility to give it up. This, too, marginalizes the family and separates the sufferers from their support system.

In addition to dividing a child from his or her family, these dysfunction-oriented theories of eating disorder origin are largely discredited and distract from getting good diagnosis and treatment. Our family did not believe that our daughter's anorexia nervosa was due to our parenting or a result of choices she was making. We came to see her illness as an involuntary attack her brain was making on her thoughts. Yet the care available to us was predicated on the assumption that her family was either unnecessary or harmful to her recovery. We could not find local therapists or eating disorder specialists that would not separate our daughter from us. We found the quality and accessibility of care to be spotty at best and at times even harmful. For that reason we chose to take primary responsibility for our daughter and to surround ourselves with resources that helped her recover.

But we cannot advocate that others follow our example. Parents should not have to do it all alone: learning about the disease, assessing their family's role, choosing treatment, and carrying out that treatment. We did it because we felt we had no other options. We are not heroes, and we are not looking for recruits.

We also have no regrets.

It is our hope that our story will encourage other parents to insist that they are included in and are an integral part of their child's treatment. We hope professionals in the field are emboldened to abandon antiquated and unsupportable ideas about eating disorders. We hope those suffering from eating disorders will receive both the physical and the emotional support they deserve.

Yet at the time I write this, resources are few for parents who would choose to actively participate in the treatment of their children. There is no organization of and for parents that advocates Maudsley-style or other family-oriented approaches. I know of no directory to guide parents to professionals with Maudsley training or orientation. Only one clinic in the United States, to my knowledge, treats eating disorders purely as brain disorders: the Kartini Clinic in Portland. Notably, Kartini actually insists that families be part of patient treatment and does not restrict parental access.

Furthermore, research results that support a medical model of eating disorders etiology are not readily available to parents, nor are the insights of the researchers gathering that data. Those that need it most are the farthest from the sources.

I look forward to a time when the treatment of eating disorders, from initial symptoms to remission, is shorter and easier for all concerned, less fraught with guilt and anger and confusion. It will most likely never be easy or simple, but we can do better. We can all do better.

PARENT TO PARENT

What I'd Say to You Over Coffee
(and a Slice of Baklava!)

Take the time to recognize and accept that an eating disorder is serious and life-threatening. It is not just going to go away.

For the present, and for a long while to come, **life must be structured around recovery**, and not the other way around.

It's not your fault. It's not your child's fault. What counts is how you react, not how you got there.

Treat the disease as an alien parasite that can be overcome but is not to be bargained with.

Food is medicine. The prescription is full nutrition, consumed and digested, every meal of every day.

It's not negotiable. Similar to insulin levels for a diabetic and chemotherapy dosages for a cancer patient, the amount a healthy body needs to eat is not negotiable. Do not bargain, do not give in.

Don't wait. Every meal, every day, all your life, starting right now.

Declare an anger-free, guilt-free, shame-free zone in your lives. Live there.

Do not give shelter to starvation, malnutrition, purging, self-harm, depressed thinking, or meanness. Make your home a safe place to be healthy.

Weigh lightly. Weight is an imperfect and tricky measure of health but up or down trends have meaning. Do it rarely, and randomly, and avoid making a fuss.

Set boundaries and maintain them. Do not allow the disease to rewrite history, rule the present, or set terms for the future.

Denial is normal, but no excuse. Patients with eating disorders are not, until later stages of treatment, rational about their illness. You need not have the sufferer's agreement to insist on treatment.

Choose your professional care wisely, as consultants but not as the ultimate authority over your child or your family.

No secrets. No subterfuge. No triangulation. Anything the parent has to say about the child to the therapist or doctors can and should be said in front of the child.

Your child doesn't "have to hit bottom." The ability to understand and fight the disease is a later stage of recovery. While physically compromised, or recovering from symptoms, people with eating disorders need a safe place to recover and people to support them.

Listen, but you don't have to agree.

Love your child all you can, with every parental muscle you have. Feel free to hate the disease, however.

Take the frightened, angry, irrational things your child says during recovery as the voice of the disease. **Forgive your child** immediately and forget the words as soon as you are able.

It is your business. An illness in the family has an impact on all its members, and family has a unique influence through what it does, and does not, do.

Consider the family as a whole in making care decisions.

Every family can find its own creative ways to support, protect, laugh, and survive a crisis.

Taking control is an act of responsible parenting, not anger or punishment.

It is not forcing them to eat, it is letting them eat—and live.

Now is the time to be a parent, not a friend. Write a letter and don't send it, call a friend and rant, hit your pillow, but your child needs your firm resolve and not another person to worry about.

Everything else is optional: nothing takes precedence over treatment. School, long-planned vacations, leaving for college, watching

TV, talking on the phone, driving the car, money, privacy—anything a parent offers beyond the bare necessities is optional.

Be united. Eating disorders strain every relationship in the family. Fight the disease, not each other.

Believe in your family, flaws and all. Trust your bravest instincts if the advice you hear does not fit.

Surround yourself with people who support your family and your decisions. Listen to them.

If you cannot make your home a place to heal, find somewhere you can. A relative's home, a hospital bed, a treatment clinic—find a place where the only thing on the menu is recovery.

There is nothing to argue about. Period.

Educate yourself. Find out for yourself what is out there to know. Get second and third opinions. Make phone calls. Read everything you can find and make up your own mind. (See the Appendix and Resources for some places to start.)

Educate others. Share what you've learned. Dispel myths.

Get care for yourself. Caregivers deserve and must have personal support. Friends, family, personal therapists, masseuses, kind neighbors, social workers, spiritual counselors—now is the time to reach out and get help.

Be specific about your needs. "A casserole a week." "Babysitting while we go to the therapist." "Listen to me cry."

Eat together. Allow your meals to be a celebration, a priority, and not an extra chore. Enjoy shopping, cooking, eating, and cleaning up together. Lose the things that get in the way.

Eat with your anorexic.

APPENDIX

History of the Maudsley Approach

WHAT IS INFORMALLY REFERRED TO as the Maudsley approach to anorexia treatment is named for the Maudsley Hospital in London, where the family-based therapy was originally developed by Christopher Dare and Ivan Eisler in the 1980s. Since then, a growing number of studies have supported the use of this method.

The role of the anorexic's family has been a hotly debated topic throughout the history of this pernicious disease, which was first named in 1874 by William Gull, an English physician. Gull called family members "the worst attendants" and banned them from the sickroom. Since its identification, treatment for anorexia has evolved but, until recently, consistently focused on separation of the ill patient from the care and influence of the family.

The Maudsley approach not only rejects the historic shunning of parents during treatment but actually embraces their involvement—putting the responsibility to feed and nourish the patient directly into the parents' hands. In addition, the home-based nature of care keeps the patient in his or her normal life and environment, allowing a gradual return to routine.

Cost, an important consideration, also differs with home-based treatment. Hospitalization of anorexia patients is notoriously expensive, and insurance rarely offers full reimbursement. In the United Kingdom,

---

BASIC PRINCIPLES OF THE MAUDSLEY APPROACH TO FAMILY-BASED TREATMENT

Anorexic patients younger than eighteen years of age who live at home are candidates for this approach.

The Maudsley model maintains an "agnostic" stand on the cause of anorexia nervosa, but notably does not assume a family was dysfunctional before the disease.

Adolescent anorexics are not considered to be in control of their behaviors; the disease itself compels them to restrict food and purge.

Parents temporarily take back control of decision making regarding food during weight restoration.

Weight restoration is the primary focus of early treatment.

Treatment, facilitated by a therapist, involves three phases:

- Refeeding
- Negotiations for a new pattern of relationships
- Adolescent issues and termination

The course of therapy is brief, usually twenty sessions over six months.

Adapted from James Lock, Daniel Le Grange, W. Stewart Agras, and Christopher Dare. 2001. *Treatment Manual for Anorexia Nervosa: A Family-Based Approach.* New York: Guilford Press.

where the Maudsley approach is part of the national health care system, home-based care is the norm and hospitalization is rare.

Recovery rates for the Maudsley approach have been estimated at 90 percent after five years, significantly higher than the 50 percent success rate usually found with standard treatment.

Dr. James Lock of Stanford University and Dr. Daniel Le Grange of the University of Chicago brought the approach to the United States in 1998, through a National Institutes of Health (NIH) treatment trial. In 2001, Lock collaborated with Le Grange, W. Stewart Agras, and Christopher Dare on the *Treatment Manual for Anorexia Nervosa*, which is now in international use. More recently, Lock and Le Grange began a five-year multisite NIH-funded study comparing individual therapy to family-based therapy, and have coauthored a book for parents, *Help Your Teenager Beat an Eating Disorder*.

The Maudsley approach is also now being examined in an NIMH randomized controlled study at the University of Chicago for use with adolescent bulimic patients.

ACKNOWLEDGMENTS

I CANNOT OVERSTATE MY GRATITUDE for the courage, generosity, and sense of humor of my daughter for allowing me to write publicly about a personal and often painful time in her life. My dear son, who is too young to understand the events described or his mother's efforts to write them down, has nevertheless contributed a steady diet of high-quality, high-energy love. My family and my husband's family have supported us fully during our difficult times and have been there to cheer during the good—it was through their example that we learned to be the best parents we can. We are very grateful to our family therapist and to Dr. Tomas Silber for their professional support. I am indebted to my "secret advisors" for their constant support and comfort and apologize for the necessity of thanking them only by initials: R.E., J.B., K.A., R.Y., P.R., K.F., L.L., K.S., A.S., D.S., C.D., K.H.W., C.V., M.A., M.J., R.J., F.B., and C.G. I have depended on and I am deeply thankful to the fellow writers who have aided me in editing the manuscript, and in particular the essayist Phyllis Theroux, for her mentorship and guidance. My agent, Bob Diforio of D4EO Literary Agency, who never seems to sleep, is any writer's dream agent. I am also deeply grateful to my editor, Michele Pezzuti, at McGraw-Hill, whose enthusiasm for our story made me feel as though I was arriving home safe from a tough journey. Finally, my admiration and thanks to my long-suffering, amazing, and amusing husband who deserves more credit for this book and my ability to write it than could be expressed in words. He has shouldered equally the weight of our family crises, but offered me the unequal gift of release through writing about it. A finer man, fellow parent, or husband I could not have found.

RESOURCES

TREATMENT CENTERS

Comprehensive Eating Disorders Program
Lucile Packard Children's Hospital
725 Welch Road
Palo Alto, CA 94304
(650) 498-4468
lpch.org/clinicalSpecialtiesServices/ClinicalSpecialties/Eating
Disorders/eatingDisordersIndex.html

Dr. James Lock's innovative program utilizing family-based treatment for anorexia

Eating Disorders Clinic
Department of Psychiatry
The University of Chicago
5841 S. Maryland Avenue
Chicago, IL 60637
(773) 702-6826
http://psychiatry.uchicago.edu/clinical/clinics/edp

Dr. Daniel Le Grange's program utilizing family-based treatment for anorexia and bulimia

New York State Psychiatric Institute
Columbia University Department of Psychiatry
Eating Disorders Research Unit
1051 Riverside Drive, Unit 98
New York, NY 10032
(212) 543-5739
eatingdisordersclinic.org
Small, free, research-oriented program

Mount Sinai Eating and Weight Disorders Program
One Gustave L. Levy Place, Box 1230
New York, NY 10029
(212) 659-8724
www.mountsinai.org/eatingdisorders
Program treats adolescents with anorexia, bulimia, and atypical eating disorders

Duke Eating Disorders Program
Box 3842
Duke University Medical Center
Durham, NC 27710
(919) 668-7301
http://eatingdisorders.mc.duke.edu
Family-based outpatient treatment with parent support groups

Kartini Clinic
2800 N. Vancouver, Suite 118
Portland, OR 97227
(503) 249-8851
kartiniclinic.com

Inpatient and intensive outpatient program that treats eating disorders as brain disorders and requires family participation in care

ONLINE RESOURCES

Academy for Eating Disorders, The (www.aedweb.org). International transdisciplinary professional organization.

Alliance for Eating Disorder Awareness, The (eatingdisorderinfo.org). Lists information, news, and treatment referral information.

ANAD—National Association of Anorexia Nervosa and Associated Disorders (anad.org). Nonprofit organization dedicated to alleviating the problems of eating disorders.

Anna Westin Foundation (www.annawestinfoundation.org). Foundation created by parents of a daughter who died at age twenty-one of anorexia.

Anorexia Nervosa and Related Eating Disorders, Inc. (ANRED) (www.anred.com). Eating disorders education and recovery information.

Cheryl Dellasega, GNP, Ph.D. (www.cheryldellasega.com). Author and parent activist, founder of Club Ophelia and Camp Ophelia.

Eating Disorders Coalition (eatingdisorderscoalition.org; 202/543-9570). Works to advance the federal recognition of eating disorders as a public health priority.

Eating Disorder Referral and Information Center (edreferral.org; 858/792-7463). Information and treatment finder.

Gurze Eating Disorders Resources (gurze.com). Over 300 books and other publications that address eating disorders, body image, and related topics.

Healthy Place (healthyplace.com). Comprehensive consumer mental health site.

International Association of Eating Disorders Professionals (www.iaedp.com). Membership directory available online.

Medline Plus Medical Dictionary (nlm.nih.gov/medlineplus/mplus dictionary.html). Searchable medical dictionary.

Medscape from WebMD (medscape.com). User-friendly searchable information.

National Eating Disorders Association (www.nationaleatingdisorders .org). National nonprofit organization offering conferences, events, and grants.

Pale Reflections Eating Disorders Community (pale-reflections .com). Information about eating disorders and treatments.

PsycCrawler (psychcrawler.com). The American Psychological Association's searchable index of media and professional news.

Psychiatry Matters (psychiatrymatters.md). A searchable digest from the United Kingdom of international psychiatric literature.

PubMed (ncbi.nlm.nih.gov/PubMed). A service of the National Library of Medicine that lists over fourteen million medical citations from the 1950s to the present.

Something Fishy (something-fishy.org). A privately owned site with information, news, online forums, and treatment finder.

BOOKS

Bryant-Waugh, Rachel, and Bryan Lask. 2004. *Eating Disorders: A Parent's Guide*. New York: Brunner-Routledge.

Dellasega, Cheryl. 2005. *The Starving Family*. Fredonia, WI: Champion Press. (Stories of families who care for children with eating disorders.)

Gremillion, Helen. 2003. *Feeding Anorexia: Gender and Power at a Treatment Center*. Durham, NC: Duke University Press.

Hendricks, Jennifer. 2003. *Slim to None: A Journey Through the Wasteland of Anorexia Treatment*. New York: McGraw-Hill.

Herrin, Marcia, and Nancy Matsumoto. 2002. *The Parent's Guide to Childhood Eating Disorders*. New York: Henry Holt.

Lock, James, and Daniel Le Grange. 2004. *Help Your Teenager Beat an Eating Disorder*. New York: Guilford Press. (A family-based guide for parents by the authors of the professional treatment manual for the Maudsley approach.)

Lock, James, Daniel Le Grange, W. Stewart Agras, and Christopher Dare. 2001. *Treatment Manual for Anorexia Nervosa: A Family-Based Approach*. New York: The Guilford Press. (The professional manual for the Maudsley approach.)

Schaefer, Jenni, and Thom Rutledge. 2003. *Life Without Ed: How One Woman Declared Independence from Her Eating Disorder and You Can Too*. New York: McGraw-Hill.

PROFESSIONAL LITERATURE

Adan, R. A., J. G. Hillenbrand, C. de Rijke, W. Nijenhuis, T. Vink, K. M. Garner, and J. H. Martien. 2003. "Melanocortin System and Eating Disorders," *Annals of the New York Academy of Sciences* 994: 267–274.

Agras, W. S., H. A. Brandt, C. M. Bulik, R. Dolan-Sewell, C. G. Fairburn, K. A. Halmi, D. B. Herzog, D. C. Jimerson, A. S. Kaplan, W. H. Kaye, D. Le Grange, J. Lock, J. E. Mitchell, M. V. Rudorfer, L. L. Street, R. Striegel-Moore, K. M. Vitonsek, B. T. Walsh, and D. E. Wilfey. 2004. "Report of the National Institutes of Health Workshop on Overcoming Barriers to Treatment Research in Anorexia Nervosa," *International Journal of Eating Disorders* 35 (4): 509–521.

Audenaert, K., K. K. Van Laere, F. Dumont, M. Vervaet, I. Goethals, G. Slegers, J. Mertens, C. van Heeringen, and R. Dierckx. 2003. "Decreased 5-HT2a Receptor Binding in Patients with Anorexia Nervosa," *Journal of Nuclear Medicine* 44 (2): 163–169.

Avraham, Y., S. Hao, S. Mendelson, and E. M. Berry. 2001. "Tyrosine Improves Appetite, Cognition, and Exercise Tolerance in Activity Anorexia," *Medicine and Science in Sports and Exercise* 33 (12): 2104–2107.

Ayton, A. K. 2004. "Dietary Polyunsaturated Fatty Acids and Anorexia Nervosa: Is There a Link?" *Nutritional Neuroscience* 7 (1): 1–12.

Baranowska, B., E. Wolinska-Witort, E. Wasilewska-Dziubinska, K. Roguski, L. Martynska, and M. Chmielowska. 2003. "The Role of Neuropeptides in the Disturbed Control of Appetite and Hormone Secretion in Eating Disorders," *Neuroendocrinology Letters* 24 (6): 431–434.

Barbarich, N. C., C. W. McConaha, K. A. Halmi, K. Gendall, S. R. Sunday, J. Gaskill, M. La Via, G. K. Frank, S. Brooks, K. H. Plotnicov, and W. H. Kaye. 2004. "Use of Nutritional Supplements to Increase the Efficacy of Fluoxetine in the Treatment of Anorexia Nervosa," *International Journal of Eating Disorders* 35 (1): 10–15.

Benini, L., T. Todesco, R. Dalle Grave, F. Deiorio, L. Salandini, and I. Vantini. 2004. "Gastric Emptying in Patients with Restricting and Binge/Purging Subtypes of Anorexia Nervosa," *American Journal of Gastroenterology* 99 (8): 1448–1454.

Ben-Tovim, David I. 2003. "Eating Disorders: Outcome, Prevention and Treatment of Eating Disorders," *Current Opinion in Psychiatry* 16 (1): 65–69.

Birmingham, C. L., E. Gutierrez, L. Jonat, and P. Beumont. 2004. "Randomized Controlled Trial of Warming in Anorexia Nervosa," *International Journal of Eating Disorders* 35 (2): 234–238.

Brown, N. W., A. Ward, R. Surwit, J. Tiller, S. Lightman, J. Treasure, and I. C. Campbell. 2003. "Evidence for Metabolic and Endocrine Abnormalities in Subjects Recovered from Anorexia Nervosa," *Metabolism* 52 (3): 296–302.

Bulik, C. M., and F. Tozzi. 2004. "Contemporary Thinking About the Role of Genes and Environment in Eating Disorders," *Epidemiologia e psichiatria sociale* 13 (2): 91–98.

Castro, J., R. Deulofeu, A. Gila, J. Puig, and J. Toro. 2004. "Persistence of Nutritional Deficiencies After Short-Term Weight Recovery in Adolescents with Anorexia Nervosa," *International Journal of Eating Disorders* 35 (2): 169–178.

Cohen, M. A., S. M. Ellis, C. W. Le Roux, R. L. Batterham, A. Park, M. Patterson, G. S. Frost, M. A. Ghatei, and S. R. Bloom. 2003. "Oxyntomodulin Suppresses Appetite and Reduces Food Intake in Humans," *Journal of Clinical Endocrinology and Metabolism* 88 (10): 4696–4701.

Ellison, Z., J. Foone, R. Howard, E. Bullmore, S. Williams, and J. Treasure. 1998. "Functional Anatomy of Calorie Fear in Anorexia Nervosa," *Lancet* 352 (9135): 1192.

Fassino, S., A. Piero, C. Gramaglia, and G. Abbate-Daga. 2004. "Clinical, Psychopathological and Personality Correlates of Interoceptive Awareness in Anorexia Nervosa, Bulimia Nervosa and Obesity," *Psychopathology* 37 (4): 168–174.

Favaro, A., L. Caregaro, L. Di Pascoli, F. Brambilla, and P. Santonastaso. 2004. "Total Serum Cholesterol and Suicidality in Anorexia Nervosa," *Psychosomatic Medicine* 66 (4): 548–552.

Favaro, A., S. Ferrara, and P. Santonastaso. 2003. "The Spectrum of Eating Disorders in Young Women: A Prevalence Study in a General Population Sample," *Psychosomatic Medicine* 65 (4): 701–708.

Fetissov, S. O., J. Hallman, L. Oreland, B. A. Klinteberg, E. Grenback, A. L. Hulting, and T. Hokfelt. 2002. "Autoantibodies Against Alpha-MSH, ACTH, and LHRH in Anorexia and Bulimia Nervosa Patients," *Proceedings of the National Academy of Sciences of the USA* 99 (26): 17155–17160.

Franko, D. L., R. H. Striegel-Moore, B. A. Barton, B. C. Schumann, D. M. Garner, S. R. Daniels, G. B. Schreiber, and P. B. Crawford. 2004. "Measuring Eating Concerns in Black and White Adolescent Girls," *International Journal of Eating Disorders* 35 (2): 179–189.

Frey, J., M. Neuhauser-Berthold, S. A. Elis, S. Duncker, F. Rose, W. F. Blum, H. Remschmidt, F. Geller, and J. Hebebrand. 2003. "Lower Serum Leptin Levels in Female Students of the Nutritional Sciences with Eating Disorders," *European Journal of Nutrition* 42 (3): 142–148.

Garner, David. 1997. "The Effects of Starvation on Behavior: Implications for Eating Disorders" in *Handbook for Treatment of Eating Disorders*, edited by D.M. Garner and P.E. Garfinkel. New York: Guilford Press, 145–177.

Gorwood, P. 2004. "Eating Disorders, Serotonin Transporter Polymorphisms and Potential Treatment Response," *American Journal of Pharmacogenomics* 4 (1): 9–17.

Gowers, S., and R. Bryant-Waugh. 2004. "Management of Child and Adolescent Eating Disorders: The Current Evidence Base and Future Directions," *Journal of Child Psychology and Psychiatry* 45 (1): 63–83.

Guisinger, Shan. 2003. "Adapted to Flee Famine: Adding an Evolutionary Perspective on Anorexia Nervosa," *Psychological Review* 110 (4): 745–61.

Hay, P., J. Bacaltchuk, A. Claudino, D. Ben-Tovim, and P. Y. Yong. 2003. "Individual Psychotherapy in the Outpatient Treatment of Adults with Anorexia Nervosa," *Cochrane Database of Systemic Reviews* (4): CD003909.

Hebebrand, J., R. Casper, J. Treasure, and U. Schweiger. 2004. "The Need to Revise the Diagnostic Criteria for Anorexia Nervosa," *Journal of Neural Transmission* 111 (7): 827–840.

Hu, X., O. Giotakis, T. Li, A. Karwautz, J. Treasure, and D. A. Collier. 2003. "Association of the 5-HT2c Gene with Susceptibility and Minimum Body Mass Index in Anorexia Nervosa," *Neuroreport* 14 (6): 781–783.

Jacobi, C., T. Paul, M. de Zwaan, D. O. Nutzinger, and B. Dahme. 2004. "Specificity of Self-Concept Disturbances in Eating Disorders," *International Journal of Eating Disorders* 35 (2): 204–210.

Johnson, Craig L., Brian C. Lund, and William R. Yates. 2003. "Recovery Rates for Anorexia Nervosa," *American Journal of Psychiatry* 160 (4): 798.

Kas, M. J., G. Van Dijk, A. J. Scheurink, and R. A. Adan. 2003. "Agouti-Related Protein Prevents Self-Starvation," *Molecular Psychiatry* 8 (2): 235–240.

Kaye, Walter, and Michael Strober. 1999. "The Neurobiology of Eating Disorders" in *Neurobiological Foundations of Mental Illness*, edited by D. S. Charney, E. J. Nestler, and B. S. Bunney. New York: Oxford University Press. 891–906.

Keel, P. K., D. J. Dorer, K. T. Eddy, D. Franko, D. L. Charatan, and D. B. Herzog. 2003. "Predictors of Mortality in Eating Disorders," *Archives of General Psychiatry* 60 (2): 179–183.

Kim, S. W., J. E. Grant, S. I. Kim, T. A. Swanson, G. A. Bernstein, W. B. Jaszcz, K. A. Williams, and P. M. Schlievert. 2004. "A Possible Association of Recurrent Streptococcal Infections and Acute Onset of Obsessive-Compulsive Disorder," *Journal of Neuropsychiatry and Clinical Neuroscience* 16: 252–260.

Kucharska-Pietura, K., V. Nikolaou, M. Masiak, and J. Treasure. 2004. "The Recognition of Emotion in the Faces and Voice of Anorexia Nervosa," *International Journal of Eating Disorders* 35 (1): 42–47.

Lacey, J. Hubert, and Clare Price. 2004. "Disturbed Families, or Families Disturbed?" *British Journal of Psychiatry* 184: 195–196.

Lawrence, A. D., J. Dowson, G. L. Foxall, R. Summerfield, T. W. Robbins, and B. J. Sahakian. 2003. "Impaired Visual Discrimination Learning in Anorexia Nervosa," *Appetite* 40 (1): 85–90.

Leidy, H. J., J. K. Gardner, B. R. Frye, M. L. Snook, M. K. Schuchert, E. L. Richard, and N. I. Williams. 2004. "Circulating Ghrelin Is Sensitive to Changes in Body Weight During a Diet and Exercise Program in Normal-Weight Young Women," *Journal of Clinical Endocrinology and Metabolism* 89 (6): 2659–2664.

Lock, J. 2002. "Treating Adolescents with Eating Disorders in the Family Context, Empirical and Theoretical Considerations," *Child and Adolescent Psychiatric Clinics of North America* 11 (2): 331–342.

Lowe, B., S. Zipfel, and C. Buchholz. 2002. "One Half of Patients with Anorexia Nervosa Fully Recovered After 21 Years but the Other Half Had a Chronic or Lethal Course," *Evidence-Based Mental Health* 5 (2): 59.

Malina, A., J. Gaskill, C. McConaha, G. K. Frank, M. LaVia, L. Scholar, and W. H. Kaye. 2003. "Olanzapine Treatment of Anorexia Nervosa: A Retrospective Study," *International Journal of Eating Disorders* 33 (2): 234–237.

Mangweth, B., A. Hausmann, T. Walch, A. Hotter, C. I. Rupp, W. Biebl, J. I. Hudson, and J. R. Pope. 2004. "Body Fat Perception in Eating-Disordered Men," *International Journal of Eating Disorders* 35 (1): 102–108.

Marcason, Wendy. 2002. "Nutrition Therapy and Eating Disorders: What Is the Correct Calorie Level for Clients with Anorexia?" *Journal of the American Dietetic Association* 102 (5): 644.

McKenzie, Jennifer, Jan Bulik, Cynthia Patrick, Fear Federica, and Tozzi Sullivan. 2003. "Causes and Recovery in Anorexia Nervosa: The Patient's Perspective," *International Journal of Eating Disorders* 33 (2): 143–154.

Miller, K. K., S. Grinspoon, S. Gleysteen, K. A. Grieco, J. Ciampa, J. Breu, D. B. Herzog, and A. Klibanski. 2004. "Preservation of Neuroendocrine Control of Reproductive Function Despite Severe Undernutrition," *Journal of Clinical Endocrinology and Metabolism* 89 (9): 4434–4438.

Munoz, M. T., and J. Argente. 2004. "New Concepts in Anorexia Nervosa," *Journal of Pediatric Endocrinology and Metabolism* 17 Suppl 3: 473–480.

Murphy, D. L., A. Lerner, G. Rudnick, and K. P. Lesch. 2004. "Serotonin Transporter: Gene, Genetic Disorders, and Pharmacogenetics," *Molecular Interventions* 4 (2): 109–123.

Nedvidkova, J., I. Dostalova, V. Bartak, H. Papezov, and K. Pacak. 2004. "Increased Subcutaneous Abdominal Tissue Norepinephrine Levels in Patients with Anorexia Nervosa: An in Vivo Microdialysis Study," *Physiological Research* 53 (4): 409–413.

Nunn, Kenneth. 2001. "'In Search of New Wineskins': The Phenomenology of Anorexia Nervosa Not Covered in DSM or ICD," *Clinical Child Psychology and Psychiatry* 6 (4): 489–503.

Pederson, K. J., J. L. Roerig, and J. E. Mitchell. 2003. "Towards the Pharmacotherapy of Eating Disorders," *Expert Opinion on Pharmacotherapy* 4 (10): 1659–1678.

Phillips, Katharine A., and Fedra Najjar. 2003. "An Open-Label Study of Citalopram in Body Dysmorphic Disorder," *Journal of Clinical Psychiatry* 64: 715–720.

Rayworth, B. B., L. A. Wise, and B. L. Harlow. 2004. "Childhood Abuse and Risk of Eating Disorders in Women," *Epidemiology* 15 (3): 271–278.

Ribases, M., M. Gratacos, F. Fernandez-Aranda, L. Bellodi, C. Boni, M. Anderluh, M. C. Cavallini, E. Cellini, D. D. Bella, S. Erzegovesi, C. Foulon, M. Gabrovsek, P. Gorwood, J. Hebebrand, A. Hinney, J. Holliday, X. Hu, and A. Karwautz. 2004. "Association of BDNF with Anorexia, Bulimia and Age of Onset of Weight Loss in Six European Populations," *Human Molecular Genetics* 13 (12): 1205–1212.

Russell, G. F., G. I. Szmukler, C. Dare, and I. Eisler. 1987. "An Evaluation of Family Therapy in Anorexia Nervosa and Bulimia Nervosa," *Archives of General Psychiatry* 44 (12): 1047–1056.

Russell, J. 2004. "Management of Anorexia Nervosa Revisited," *British Medical Journal* 328 (7438): 479–480.

Schmidt, U. H., N. A. Troop, and J. Treasure. 1999. "Events and the Onset of Eating Disorders: Correcting an 'Age Old' Myth," *International Journal of Eating Disorders* 25 (1): 83–88.

Segal, A., D. Kinoshita Kussunoki, and M. Aparecida Larino. 2004. "Post-Surgical Refusal to Eat: Anorexia Nervosa, Bulimia Nervosa or a New Eating Disorder? A Case Series," *Obesity Surgery* 14 (3): 353–360.

Siegfried, Z., K. Kanyas, Y. Latzer, O. Karni, M. Bloch, B. Lerer, and E. M. Berry. 2004. "Association Study of Cannabinoid Receptor Gene (CNR1) Alleles and Anorexia Nervosa: Differences Between Restricting and Binging/Purging Subtypes," *American Journal of Medical Genetics* 125B (1): 126–130.

Sodersten, P., C. Bergh, and A. Ammar. 2003. "Anorexia Nervosa: Towards a Neurobiologically Based Therapy," *European Journal of Pharmacology* 480 (1–3): 67–74.

Sohler, N. L., E. J. Bromet, J. Lavelle, T. J. Craig, and R. Mojtabai. 2004. "Are There Racial Differences in the Way Patients with Psychotic Disorders Are Treated at Their First Hospitalization?" *Psychological Medicine* 34 (4): 705–718.

Stamatakis, E. A., and M. M. Hetherington. 2003. "Neuroimaging in Eating Disorders," *Nutritional Neuroscience* 6 (6): 325–34.

Steiger, H. 2004. "Eating Disorders and the Serotonin Connection: State, Trait and Developmental Effects," *Journal of Psychiatry and Neuroscience* 29 (1): 20–29.

Striegel-Moore, Ruth H., Faith A. Dohm, Helena C. Kraemer, C. Barr Taylor, Stephen Daniels, Patricia B. Crawford, and George B. Schreiber. 2003. "Eating Disorders in White and Black Women," *American Journal of Psychiatry* 160: 1326–1331.

Strober, M. 2004. "Pathologic Fear Conditioning and Anorexia Nervosa: On the Search for Novel Paradigms," *International Journal of Eating Disorders* 35 (4): 504–508.

Su, J. C., and C. L. Birmingham. 2002. "Zinc Supplementation in the Treatment of Anorexia Nervosa," *Eating and Weight Disorders* 7 (1): 20–22.

Tagami, T., N. Satoh, T. Usui, K. Yamada, A. Shimatsu, and H. Kuzuya. 2004. "Adiponectin in Anorexia Nervosa and Bulimia Nervosa," *Journal of Clinical Endocrinology and Metabolism* 89 (4): 1833–1837.

Tanaka, Muneki, Yoshiki Tatebe, et. al. 2003. "Eating Pattern and the Effect of Oral Glucose on Ghrelin and Insulin Secretion in Patients with Anorexia Nervosa," *Clinical Endocrinology* 59 (5): 574–579.

Tannhauser, P. P. 2002. "Anorexia Nervosa: A Multifactorial Disease of Nutritional Origin?" *International Journal of Adolescent Medicine and Health* 14 (3): 185–91.

Toth, E., F. Tury, A. Gati, J. Weisz, I. Kondakor, and M. Molnar. 2004. "Effects of Sweet and Bitter Gustatory Stimuli in Anorexia Nervosa on EEG Frequency Spectra," *International Journal of Psychophysiology* 52 (3): 285–290.

Ueta, Yoichi, Yumi Ozaki, Jun Saito, and Tatsushi Onaka. 2003. "Involvement of Novel Feeding-Related Peptides in Neuroendocrine Response to Stress," *Experimental Biology and Medicine* 228: 1168–1174.

Uher, R., M. J. Brammer, T. Murphy, I. C. Campbell, V. W. Ng, S. C. Williams, and J. Treasure. 2003. "Recovery and Chronicity in Anorexia Nervosa: Brain Activity Associated with Differential Outcomes," *Biological Psychiatry* 54 (9): 934–942.

Uher, R., T. Murphy, M. J. Brammer, T. Dalgleish, M. L. Phillips, V. W. Ng, C. M. Andrew, S. C. Williams, I. C. Campbell, and J. Treasure. 2004. "Medial Prefrontal Cortex Activity Associated with Symptom Provocation in Eating Disorders," *American Journal of Psychiatry* 161 (7): 1238–1246.

Vandereycken, W. 2003. "The Place of Inpatient Care in the Treatment of Anorexia Nervosa: Questions to Be Answered," *International Journal of Eating Disorders* 34 (4): 409–422.

Vedantam, Shankar. 2003. "Study: Thousands Give Up Children to Get Care," *Washington Post*, April 22, 2003, A2.

Wade, T. D., J. Wilkinson, and D. Ben-Tovim. 2003. "The Genetic Epidemiology of Body Attitudes, the Attitudinal Component of Body Image in Women," *Psychological Medicine* 33 (8): 1395–1405.

Ward, A., J. Tiller, J. Treasure, and J. Russell. 2000. "Eating Disorders: Psyche or Soma?" *International Journal of Eating Disorders* 27 (3): 279–287.

Wolfe, B. E., D. C. Jimerson, C. Orlova, and C. S. Mantzoros. 2004. "Effect of Dieting on Plasma Leptin, Soluble Leptin Receptor, Adiponectin and Resistin Levels in Healthy Volunteers," *Clinical Endocrinology* 61 (3): 332–338.

Yasuhara, D., S. Kojima, S. Nozoe, and T. Naruo. 2004. "Intense Fear of Caloric Intake Related to Severe Hypoglycemia in Anorexia Nervosa," *General Hospital Psychiatry* 26 (3): 243–245.